Fallen

OUT OF THE SEX INDUSTRY AND
INTO THE ARMS OF THE SAVIOR

Annie Lobert

WORTHY®
PUBLISHING

Library of Congress Control Number: 2014957120

To Jesus Christ, who redeemed and rescued me.

*To my husband, Oz Fox, for loving me
and never being intimidated by my past.*

*To my family and all my friends, past and present, who
have been with me on my incredible journey to wholeness.*

*To all those who are still out there lost and
looking for a way home. If you keep searching,
you will find your way. Never give up.*

CONTENTS

Prologue   *"Break Yourself!"* .... *ix*

Chapter 1   Little Girl Lost 1

Chapter 2   Fallen Arises 17

Chapter 3   He Who Sold Me a Dream 41

Chapter 4   Broken Wings 55

Chapter 5   The Pimp Game 69

Chapter 6   Runaway Girl 93

Chapter 7   Renegade 119

Chapter 8   Glorious Disaster 137

Chapter 9   Learning to Fly 155

Chapter 10   Arms Wide Open 175

Chapter 11   Freed to Set Others Free 189

Chapter 12   My Dream Come True 199

Appendix A   *What Is Sex Trafficking?* *209*

Appendix B   *Testimonials from Destiny House* *217*

Acknowledgments *225*

"BREAK YOURSELF!"

A beating is all it took. An hour of fury unleashed, blood splattering onto the sparkling white floor while my boyfriend-turned-pimp smashed my head repeatedly into the kitchen cabinets.

"Break yourself!" he demanded. In other words, "hand over the money." The money I had just made turning tricks on the Las Vegas Strip. As his hands clutched my throat, his nails marking my skin, my defiant cries for him to stop turned into desperate gasps for breath. The punches ensued, and I blacked out.

I drifted in and out of consciousness, coming to while being choked and punched in my face and ribs. Another blow by his large fist knocked me out. When I opened my eyes the next time, I was lying facedown in a pile of fresh dog feces in the backyard. Mixed with the tears that streamed down my face, the blood on my face ran pink, leaving a putrid taste in my mouth.

Though likely suffering a concussion, I tried to regain my bearings. My vision blurred between the tears and the feces, I saw the man I was in love with. Drops of blood stained his stark white shirt, his eyes full of rage. "You're lucky to be with me, let alone be alive! I won't be having any disrespectful attitude!" he screamed with a flurry of obscenities. "I love you! Don't you know that?! Wipe them tears off your face and shut up before I take you out to the desert and bury you six feet under! This is pimpin'! Imma be your boss from now on!"

My worst fears had come true. The man I had given my heart to really was a pimp. It was official. I had been broken. In pimp culture, that meant I now worked for him as his slave and would have to hand over every dollar I earned. That night I found myself in the game. Green, wet behind the ears, I would learn the rules as I played, breaking them at times and almost paying for the lapses with my life.

I lay on the ground practically lifeless, my nostrils filling with the reeking stench of patched grass, feces, and blood, the metallic taste dripping down my throat. I could hear my now-pimp continuing his rant of obscenities. As his berating monologue trailed off, I waited to wake up. *Surely this is a dream, and any moment now it'll be over. Oh dear God, please let me wake up, I'm begging You!*

Only it wasn't. It was just the beginning.

Out in the backyard of my best friend's house in Sin City, getting the living daylights beaten out of me, I thought of simpler times. Home. Winters spent making angels in the deep, thick Minnesota snow. Summers on my bike, dipping up and down steep and winding country roads. My parents, who had worked hard and had done their best to raise me right.

What had happened to me? How on earth did I find myself bound to a pimp who demanded my obedience and loyalty by attempting to beat the very life out of me? I had wanted to escape this life before, but now I felt trapped.

CHAPTER 1

LITTLE GIRL LOST

*"When one's lost, I suppose it's good advice to stay where
you are, until someone finds you. But who'd ever think to
look for me here?"*
—Alice in *Alice in Wonderland*

I entered the world on September 26, 1967, in southern Minneapolis, during the summer of love. Bell-bottoms ruled, miniskirts were the rage, mood rings were hip, Twiggy was queen, and the Beatles and the Doors blared.

I'll always consider myself a Minnesota girl, even though we lived in Illinois and Wisconsin as well. Because we moved around a lot, I was the "new girl" most of my young life, with my sense of security stripped away wherever I went. As difficult as that was, a part of me liked creating adventures in new places—from the turkey farm echoing with incessant gobbling to a brownstone-lined suburb of Chicago to a house next door to a synagogue where deeply religious Jews showed us compassion many times over when we were in need.

I loved my mama, Joann, dearly. Raised Catholic, she came from a large Polish family of nine siblings. As a little girl, I was attached to her at the hip. Wherever she went, I followed on her heels, sometimes even hanging on to her purse straps to make sure she was close. She made me feel safe when I was around her. We could talk about anything, and I knew that she always had my best interest at heart. I felt genuinely loved through her gentle grace and kindness.

My father, Chet, on the other hand, was not so gentle and kind. Dad served in the air force for a few years, and his personality reflected the strict, regimented military lifestyle. Originally from Chicago and of German and French descent, his roots trace back to Amsterdam, home of the famous red light district.

My sister, Diane, was the firstborn, and she took to her part well. She was smart, artistic, played the piano, and knew how to sew and cook. I looked up to Diane, who always did the right thing, but I was sometimes envious of her. I never forgot the comparisons my mom and dad would occasionally make about the two of us.

Unbeknownst to my family at the time, my sister was born with Marfan syndrome, a genetic disorder that affects the body's connective tissue and causes rapid and excessive growth; we just thought she was unusually skinny and tall. Diane was teased a lot growing up. The kids nicknamed her "Buck Teeth" because of her overbite and "Bean Pole" because she was so thin. I often stuck up for her, regardless of my resentment toward her, because I knew what a great person she was. After all, she was my sis!

My brother Bill was almost two years older than I, and he was my protector. If anyone tried to give me a hard time as a kid, he would always step in and stop it. My little brother, Charlie, is

two years younger than I and was a big clown who loved insti-
gating trouble. He made life fun with his wild ways and playful
personality. He would sometimes mercilessly pick dumb fights
with me while Bill would sweep in like a knight in shining armor
to rescue me and save the day. We Lobert kids loved each other.
Though we had our share of typical sibling rivalry and conflicts,
we were as thick as thieves.

Dad was the disciplinarian in the family. He had a deep,
powerful voice that carried throughout the house. Whenever
he yelled, I stopped dead in my tracks, whether I was skid-
ding on the kitchen floor in my dirty socks or playing with my
Barbie dolls in my room. His anger frightened me. Since I can
remember, I was deathly afraid of making him mad.

If we kids didn't follow through with a task or chore
according to what he considered was the right way, well, there
was serious hell to pay. Out would come the forked leather
belt, the end intentionally cut into straps. Like most parents
of that generation, my father instilled the fear of beatings into
us, the punishment for sassing, getting out of line, or rough-
housing. While my brothers bore the brunt of Dad's physical anger, I was always worried that I would be next in line.
It seemed I was forever waiting my turn.

———•———

While living in Minneapolis, my mom took us to church
every Sunday. I enjoyed Sunday school because the teachers
passed out candy and cupcakes, but the preaching during the
service was long and boring. Week after week, the preacher's
words strung together hypnotically and many times would make

me fall asleep. The only time I sat up and paid close attention was during Christmas Eve services. I felt something pure and perfect, completely peaceful, during those services. Perhaps it was the presence of God. I would feel it so deeply and would cry when the choir sang melodies like "Ave Maria" and "Silent Night," because I knew instinctively there was good in the world. There just *had* to be. Jesus saw me and what I was going through. He had come to make all the wrongs done to me right.

I remember countless times watching tears stream down Mama's face during the last lackluster hymn on a regular Sunday right before the service concluded. "Mama," I would whisper, tugging the hem of her flowery print dress. "Why are you crying?" She would turn to me, a sadness in her eyes, and whisper back, "Hush now, Annie, be a good girl." I felt so bad for her. I could see she was deeply anguished. I didn't know what made her so upset, but I wanted to fix it.

I wondered if she cried because of Daddy. I knew his rage well. My father's violent behavior, his intimidating, booming voice, his insistence on harsh discipline—all those things caused me to fear him. Not only that, my memory would flash back to images of my dad yelling at my mom and punching her in the nose or eye to punish her for arguing with him. When he hit her I felt so bad for her . . . powerless and helpless. I tried to distance myself from him, spending a lot of time in my room under my bed or hanging outside with my friends. When I was around him, I walked on eggshells, careful not to do anything to make him angry.

We had a bittersweet relationship. While I was extremely afraid of Daddy, I still longed for him to accept and love me. After all, I loved him, no matter what he did. I really did. And

I thought if I was good enough, I could make him happy and finally earn his love.

Dad's words had a hold over me, and usually the things he said weren't so nice. I remember hanging out at the first Target in town with my friends when I was eight years old. On a dare, I stole some plastic toy Barbie shoes, stuffing my pockets full of the tiny high heels. Nervous and scared walking out of Target and into the parking lot, I was tapped on the shoulder. I turned around to look and my stomach instantly felt ill. I was apprehended by a security guard, who to me looked like Jesus, if Jesus happened to be a hippie with glasses and long hair. When I got home, I had to tell my father what had happened. I will never forget how afraid I was because I knew the punishment that was coming.

His words stung. "So you're a thief now? Why would you do something like that? What a bad little girl. Shame on you, Annie! Stupid girl!"

Surprisingly, I didn't get a severe whooping. My punishment was worse. Dad grounded me for a full thirty days. The worst part was that it was in the middle of summer vacation! I wasn't allowed to leave the house, not even to go into the backyard to play. Every night as I rested my head on my pillow, I felt the guilt and shame of his words cover me with more weight than my heavy blanket.

Thief.

Bad.

Stupid.

Throughout my childhood, I was lost in my father's anger, unsure of his love for me. I felt disconnected from him, and always hoped that maybe someday a bond would develop.

The absence of love I felt from my father growing up left a life-sized hole in my heart that I became quite adept at trying to fill—usually with all the wrong things.

Years later, as an adult, I visited my parents in Wisconsin on Christmas, with the hopes of telling my dad I forgave him for how he treated me growing up. I had a deep sense of how important it was to do, not for him, but for me. It was part of my healing process. But as I opened my mouth to tell him, my dad bowed his head slightly and said, barely above a whisper, "Annie, I need to tell you something. I need to ask you to forgive me. I didn't treat you right growing up. My dad raised me pretty rough. He did things to me I can't talk about right now. I didn't know how to be a father. And I'm sorry." My father's voice trembled as tears slid down the face of a man I had rarely seen cry.

My tears joined his, and I reached out for his hand, rough from years of manual labor, worn from age and hard work. I held his hand as the stillness of the holy moment consumed us. I didn't even have to broach the topic. I didn't have to say a word. Dad said it all. And all the years of harshness, of feeling disconnected from him, of feeling unloved, unraveled in truth. Hurt people hurt people. And I finally understood why he acted the way he did—he was abused harshly as a child by my grandfather.

Don't get me wrong. I always loved my dad. I saw the good in him. I knew how much fun he could be. Sometimes he'd play games with us, his bellowing voice softened by hearty laughter. He would take us on fishing and camping adventures to lakes up north in Minnesota and Wisconsin. Other times he'd take us on wild rides on our snowmobiles in the cold and snowy

Minnesota winters and hit the four-wheelers when spring and summer came. We always got the latest toys before the other kids in town. I thought it was strange because we didn't have much money, certainly nothing extra we could afford to spend on frivolous things. What I didn't know was that he was depleting his retirement account with those purchases. Maybe it was a way to relieve the guilt he felt for being harsh with us.

Guilt makes you do funny things. It's a powerful emotion that changes how you look at, react, and respond to people, situations, and life. Guilt that stems from a place of confusion is a tricky thing. While it may not be legitimate, it can still shape you. And it can create in you a shame that grows and festers for years.

———•———

When I was nine years old, I hung out with a girl a few years older than me from my school. Every now and then I'd spend the night. We'd watch TV way past midnight, shovel popcorn in our mouths, and talk about nothing too important— you know, little-girl stuff.

On one particular sleepover, I woke up early one morning and found her on top of me, groping my body. No more little-girl stuff. I was shocked, grossed out. I didn't know exactly what she was doing; I just knew it made me feel awkward and uncomfortable. "I don't want to do that," I said, wrangling my body out from under hers. My friend just shrugged and began talking about her record collection.

I was so embarrassed, and I didn't want to make a big deal about it. I tried to forget about it, hoping it was an isolated incident. But something similar happened weeks later. And then again. I was so confused. She was my friend, yet I felt violated. I was afraid to tell anyone, and the guilt consumed me. I blamed myself for what happened and wondered if God could ever forgive me. I decided then that I was a dirty little girl, undeserving of redemption. I carried the shame with me over the years, blaming myself time after time when others mistreated or even abused me. I felt responsible. The instinctive voice in my head said it was always my fault.

At the time of the abuse, I began attending a Lutheran parochial school. My previous elementary school had closed down, and my father didn't like the neighborhood the new school was in. My parents had enrolled me in what I was sure would be a stuffy eight-hour bore fest, given my church experience. I was gloriously wrong.

There I discovered a faith rooted in love and joy. My teacher, Miss Barbara, glowed with something special that I couldn't quite figure out at first. Then I realized what it was. She was never worried. She never seemed to have a bad day. She had peace, and always wore a genuine smile. I wanted to be like her, happy, confident, and full of joy. She would play the guitar in class and sing songs. The first one I ever learned was "I got the joy-joy-joy-joy down in my heart." With sweet kindness in her eyes, she shared how Jesus was my friend and loved me so much, and that there wasn't anything or anybody who could stop Him from loving me.

Seeds were planted. I wanted the kind of love that Miss Barbara spoke of, the kind of love it was evident she felt. I started to believe that Jesus loved me, that it was possible to be loved, even when I wasn't perfect and I messed up. However, that small sense of inner security would sadly be ripped away whenever the neighborhood girl made sexual advances.

I had my first real crush when I was nine, and I was pretty sure I was going to go steady with him. As far as I was concerned, I was all grown up and knew what I was doing. He was the first boy to hold my hand, the first to share a kiss. My ecstasy at finding true love was short-lived, however, as my parents had to pull me out of the school because they couldn't afford the tuition any longer.

Crushing on that kid revealed my deep-rooted desire for love, for a fairy tale. It was in my bones. Disney movies established a precedent for my romantic expectations—specifically the part about falling in love and living happily ever after. That whimsical notion was the focus of every movie I watched and consequently became the goal of my life. I was Cinderella. I knew there was a fancy life-changing ball that I was going to be invited to one day. How hard could it be, right?

I wanted my prince. I needed him. I pined after the image of a well-dressed, handsome, smart guy who would buy me roses and sweep me off my feet. I think those unrealistic expectations set the stage for me to become boy crazy in my preteen years. I constantly giggled around boys and craved their attention. I mean, it was all about the boys! I'd get butterflies in my stomach when a cute guy would smile approvingly at me or dole out a compliment.

———•———

Right before I entered the sixth grade, we moved to Balsam Lake, Wisconsin, a little country town about seventy miles from Minneapolis. My parents had bought property there a few years earlier, and Dad wanted out of the city because his job was stressing him out. He loved the country life, the peaceful setting of the great outdoors, the pace of farmers who weren't bound by time clocks and demanding bosses. I didn't want to move. I finally had established some roots in Minneapolis. I had friends. I knew all the kids in the neighborhood, and everyone knew me.

For the first six months, we lived in a trailer without running water while my dad and brothers built our new home. We had to shower at our neighbors' down the road. I hated it. It was embarrassing and inconvenient, and once again I was the new girl on the block, but this time I lived way out in the country and had to ride a bus for over an hour just to get to the middle school.

The kids there were stuck up, and the pressure to fit in was overwhelming, especially because I was in a physically awkward stage. I was flat as a board, but my mom took me shopping for a bra anyway. Could life get any worse? I hated school, but I didn't hate boys. And the few girlfriends I had just added to the problem because we were constantly talking about cute boys we thought we were in love with.

I did hate being picked last in gym class. Hated when teachers called on me and I would get tongue-tied, tripping up my words. Hated when I was made fun of because I didn't wear cool layered polo shirts, boat shoes, or turtlenecks with specks of stars and hearts on them like the popular girls did. I hated being called ugly names by girls and getting pushed and punched in the stomach by boys (whom I later found out had crushes on me). Basically I hated the way I was treated at school. I felt unlovable and was convinced there was something seriously wrong with me.

My one escape was music. I could play the piano by ear since I was five. And in the eighth grade, I taught myself how to play the guitar, plucking away on a cheap acoustic my sister had found at a yard sale. I would hear songs on the radio and strum along. At night I'd listen to the lulling sounds of classical music on my Walkman, floating away on the heavenly melodies of Mozart and Handel. I loved music. And yet, not even the classics could soothe my pain. I had so much pent-up angst that was dying to escape.

I know now this is unfair to my dad, but at the time I resented him. I resented him for spending money to build up his antique collection while making me shop at garage sales or the local church basement for my outfits. I resented him for not understanding how important it was for me to fit in with all the cool kids. I resented not being able to participate in after-school activities because we lived too far away and didn't have the money for it anyway. Dad tried his best—I know that now—but somewhere between the resentment I felt toward him and the exhausting climb to try to win his approval, I snapped. I figured I might as well try the bad route but keep it quiet, like a secret rebellion. Because the good route wasn't getting me anywhere I wanted to be.

I started stealing Dad and Mom's cigarettes. My friends and I would hightail it into the woods on our three-wheelers and smoke in secret, hanging out on a hill overlooking our property. Cigarette dangling from my mouth, I'd peer through a small clearing amid the dense grove of red pine trees, puffing out circles of smoke (I didn't inhale yet), and watch Dad work on the house below. I felt a sense of satisfaction, doing something behind his back. *Look at me, Dad. Look at what I'm doing. Oh wait, you can't. Nah-nah-nah-nah-nah.* My parents never knew I smoked. Perfume and gum masked the telltale odor.

Taking a cue from Daisy Mae Dukes, the sexy character from the original *Dukes of Hazzard* show, I started slicing off my jeans and wore the shortest cutoffs possible. The higher my shorts, the happier I was. I was proud of my super lean body. I rode my bike constantly along the hilly country roads so my legs were thin but muscular. On one hand, I had no problem showing off my physique; on the other hand, I never felt thin enough. I was always on a diet. I was also a part-time bulimic. Fearing that I would gain a pound, I would sneak into the bathroom and discard food if I felt too full after I ate. The scale became my best friend and my worst enemy. I'd obsessively step on it five to ten times a day, my eyes glued to the red dial as it jiggled furiously to its resting place, to what I hoped would be a skinny number.

There was something to be said about the way I looked and the attention it commanded. I would walk down the country roads of Wisconsin with my friends and wave at men, young and old alike, driving in their cars. Sometimes I even boldly flashed cars that whooshed by just to see what kind of reaction I would get. It was exhilarating. The attention from the opposite sex gave me a thrill like no other. It boosted my confidence, and my self-esteem soared. I felt proud, beautiful, wanted. This was a new feeling I craved and wanted more of.

I was in the ninth grade, right before our final move to another town, when I was sexually abused again. A cute senior liked me. He was older, mature, and, boy, was I spellbound by his sweet words and warm kisses. He would pick me up at the house and we'd go for long drives, stopping atop scenic hills to make out. One afternoon he slid his hands down my pants. I was taken aback and embarrassed, but afraid to push him away or say no. I truly believed if I let him have his way, he would like me even more. It was such a pattern—doing things I really didn't want to do because I thought it was the only way I'd ever experience love. I was crushed and confused the next day when he left a note for me on my school locker saying he never wanted to see me again.

I thought he liked me. I thought letting him touch me would guarantee a relationship. I should have learned my lesson, but I continued to act out in different ways and with different men.

When we moved to Frederick, thirty miles away, I was determined to fit in, so I joined as many after-school activities as I could (although that was short-lived because I didn't have a way to get home) and regularly attended parties following football and basketball games to smoke cigarettes and drink beer with all the cool kids. And then I met my first real boyfriend.

Jake was a gorgeous football player, and I was smitten. I had found my prince. We fell in love hard and fast. Jake was a master at pulling my heartstrings and knew exactly how to woo me into romantic oblivion, surprising me with red roses at the most random times and showering me with sweet compliments while looking deep into my eyes with his dreamy blue eyes.

It wasn't long before he told me he loved me and wanted to consummate our relationship with sex. I wasn't ready yet. When I told him, he freaked out and put the pressure on, but

I wouldn't budge. I needed time. I can't remember who initiated the breakup, but it happened. And I was devastated.

A few weeks later I agreed to go with a girlfriend of mine to a keg party after a football game one night. I got drunk. Some guy I vaguely remember, who was in his early twenties, started flirting with me and led me upstairs to a dark bedroom. In a matter of a few blurry seconds, he pushed me down on the bed and grabbed the top of my pants, roughly pulling them down to my ankles with a force that shocked me. As inebriated as I was, I lashed out at him with my fingernails and began to claw whatever flesh my hands could touch. When I heard the rip of a condom package opening and the unzipping of his jeans, I screamed and fought my way out of his strong grip, continuing to claw his chest. My heart pounded as I ran out of the room, down the stairs, and through the crowd of teenage partiers who were dancing. With shaking hands, I pulled my girlfriend Jennifer out of the intoxicated mob and whispered, "Someone just tried to rape me."

She drove me home, dumbfounded, as I sat in silence and numbly fixed my sight ahead. I felt a familiar sense of guilt wash over me. I closed my eyes, trying to stuff away the fuzzy memory of a stranger forcing himself on me, but the voices of shame echoing in my heart only grew louder. *It's my fault. I deserved the attempted rape.* I didn't tell another soul, and as days passed into weeks, I became better at pretending, ignoring the violation, pressing it further back into my memory until only broken bits remained.

Jake and I ended up getting back together, and by then I was ready, willing, and able to give him what he wanted. Making love to him for the first time was a special moment to me. I looked at my virginity as a gift, and I thought that by giving Jake this piece of me, I would keep him, that a part of him would always remain connected to me.

Young love is manipulative, full of lies that can easily poison a naive and desperate heart. It tricks you into thinking it will last forever, that the one you love is the only one for you, that you will marry him, have cute babies who never cry, and live a perfect white-picket-fence life. It's magic, complete with castles, pixie dust, and fairy tales. I was convinced Jake and I were the real deal. Then I learned he was cheating on me with three different girls. I was devastated. My heart cried, *But he promised this was forever!* Jake didn't deny or confirm my accusations. He just looked at me with no expression whatsoever and said, "Well, let's break up then." His apathy hit me hard. I cried myself to sleep every night for weeks.

Once I allowed the sadness its due, though, I became hell-bent on getting my groove back by drinking a bit more at parties, smoking pot, and finding another boyfriend. And even though I was looking for love, a hardness of heart developed as time went by, with more failed relationships and more sexual abuse. I was embittered by men, determined not to let another one hurt me like Jake had ever again.

I graduated from high school in 1986 with a huge chip on my shoulder. The pain of betrayal and continuing absence of paternal affection snowballed into this hunger for revenge. I made it my mission to be successful, to show everyone I believed robbed me of my happiness who the real boss was. I couldn't wait to get the heck out of that little town in Wisconsin.

I made plans to stay with my sister, Diane, in her tiny two-bedroom basement apartment, a mere seven blocks from bustling downtown Minneapolis. I had thought about college, but it didn't seem like it was going to happen. My parents neither encouraged nor dissuaded me going to school. They certainly didn't have the cash to pay my tuition. So I determined to work, save up money, and eventually go to college. Then I'd become a successful business chick and make big money. I would become the prettiest, the smartest, and the fastest woman around the track.

The week after graduation I said tearful good-byes to all my girlfriends and family. My grandfather picked me up in his white Chevy Malibu. As we rode down the driveway, I whipped my neck around to see Mom and Dad waving. As they got smaller and smaller in the distance, I saw my mother wipe away tears. I couldn't hold in my emotions any longer and let the stream of tears fall down my face as my parents became mere black specks. And then they were gone.

I can't explain it. I knew in my heart I'd never be back, but the ache I felt for the loss was tempered by the sense of freedom deep in my soul. My life was now a blank slate. I wanted to be somebody. I wanted power, not to be squashed as a helpless victim.

World, here I come.

CHAPTER 2

FALLEN ARISES

"God has given you one face,
and you make yourself another."
—William Shakespeare

I was so excited to head out into the world and make my life an adventurous success. I knew my future would bring true happiness, accomplishment, fulfillment . . . and love.

The freedom of being on my own was invigorating. I felt like the chains had been cut off my feet and hands. My new life was awesome! I could do what I wanted, when I wanted. No curfew. No dad breathing down my neck. No mandatory chore list. No roaring demands to make my bed (though my sister would repeatedly and very lovingly remind me to rinse out my dishes in the sink).

I hit the ground running, looking for work in the clerical field so I could stash away enough for school or even for some music courses. Within five days of moving to Minneapolis, searching the want ads in the local paper and making phone calls, I found work. From 7:40 a.m. until 4:40 p.m., Monday through Friday, I worked downtown at Investors Diversified Services (IDS), a subsidiary of American Express, in the accounting department. I absolutely loved going into work. My office was in the tallest building in all of Minnesota, standing at an impressive 190 feet. Through the glass revolving doors constantly cycled serious-faced male and female executives wearing sharp suits and carrying leather briefcases. I felt like I was working in the heartbeat of the city. In the maze of the corporate skyscrapers, gourmet restaurants, and luxury department stores that catered to the sophisticated, I felt pretty darn important.

Day after day, I sat in my cubicle staring at the screen of a bulky beige-colored computer while combing through insurance policies. I worked hard and was good at what I did. I definitely enjoyed the perks of the company. They offered free health insurance, company shares, and even paid for my car insurance.

Inspired by TV shows like *Dynasty* and *Dallas*, I looked the part in the corporate world. I loved to power-dress and wore square-shouldered suits or blazers and colorful pumps that always matched my handbags. My hair was high and stiff, and the jewelry I wore was just as bright and bold. I'll admit; I had a bit of a spending problem. I blew most of my first paycheck on clothes. I'd try to restrain myself on future paydays, saving up some money to eventually get my own place and, of course, spend the extra on nice outfits. After all, I didn't get to have new clothes very often growing up—they were mostly from garage sales. Back then, image was everything. Looking good and put together would attract acceptance and respect, two things I craved and desperately needed in addition, of course, to love.

A few nights a week I moonlighted at Ichiban, a Japanese steakhouse and sushi bar about ten blocks and a quick bus ride away from IDS. Wearing a traditional Japanese kimono, I served teppanyaki to the customers. On the weekends I waited at Dulono's Pizza, a biker bar that served the best pizza in town.

I worked hard and played just as hard. A childhood friend had introduced me to a beautiful girl named Kimmie, who had long brown hair, a stunning million-dollar smile, and a charming and bubbly personality. We clicked immediately and became best friends. When I had a day off, we'd party and hit the clubs. Carrie, a childhood friend who also lived in the city, and I would crash the frat parties at the University of Minnesota in hopes of meeting guys who were on their way to becoming somebodies, their education catapulting them into big-time moneymaking careers.

While Carrie and I never got carded at the college parties, Kimmie and I would have to sneak or flirt our way into the downtown rock clubs like First Avenue (where Prince got his start), Uptown, and Marshall's. There, we let off steam to the sounds of Depeche Mode, Robert Palmer, Run DMC, Alexander O'Neil, Salt-N-Pepa, and Prince while shooting back Long Island iced teas. I also started hanging around the local musicians. I loved all forms of music, but was mostly drawn to soft rock, R&B, pop, and funk. I made some pretty strong connections with some of the local bands, and a few months down the road started doing some vocal studio work.

The university parties were wild, a blur of beer and inebriated students. One night at a frat house party, I was drunk and went upstairs to find a bathroom. A guy was following me, but I didn't see him until I stumbled into a bedroom. I thought I had just clumsily tripped on some empty Budweiser cans until I found myself lying on an unmade bed with a guy I had never seen standing over me. He looked at me as he turned up the volume on a radio playing Top Forty songs, and then he ripped my yellow sundress off and began to rape me. It happened so fast. Bits and pieces remain in my mind today. I'll never forget how dirty I felt. And responsible. *It's my fault. I asked for it. I made him do it.*

I don't mean to sound detached as I write these events. They were traumatic. Disgusting. Hurtful and shameful. I tried hard to block out some of them as if they never happened, but it was a destructive pattern that kept repeating.

A few weeks later I woke up one morning in an unfamiliar bed. As the blinding sunlight streamed through the panoramic window of a high-rise condo, I panicked, not knowing where I was. I furiously tried to untangle myself from a twisted web of black satin sheets. The first step I took was pain-filled, my private parts so sore I almost fell flat on my face. I saw a man in the bathroom, shaving. He looked familiar. As scenes from a club the night before surfaced in a fuzzy sea of random snap-shots, my head began to pound. He was a famous local music producer, a man I'd been introduced to by a friend.

He seemed oblivious to my disorientation and panic. "What did you do to me last night?" I cried out, partly from fear and partly from the unbearable pain I was feeling. As my mind stumbled through the shadowy memory of the previous night, I started to recall more details about him. I gasped to myself when I remembered his other occupation as a prominent local drug dealer. The guy looked at me, unfazed, and smiled. "Girl, you know you wanted it."

Choking back tears, I furiously gathered up my belong-ings that were scattered all over the stark bedroom and made a beeline for the door. I left the condo feeling dirty and ashamed, which was sadly becoming commonplace.

I dated during this time, going in and out of short-term relationships. I thought of myself as a romantic, but you could have called me a love addict. I fell hard and fast for the men I met, giving away my heart easily and quickly. There was the one sweet musician who totally trashed my heart, the other musician I said good-bye to, the steamy romance with the air force guy from the gym who moved away to California, and many others. I was always crushing on someone.

I was a sucker for love, for wild and adventurous romance. And I thought if I could do the right things or look the right part, I could attract a guy and ultimately win his love forever. Problem is, I started realizing that the perfect man, even the perfect romance, could sour—and usually did. And once the fire dampened, I stood alone in my dark and lonely castle of love gone wrong, fielding the blame every time.

When a guy lost interest in me or moved on to someone else or did something so simple like not return my phone call, I determined it was my fault. There was always something wrong with me, and these thoughts continually crept into my mind: *I like him too much. I was too aloof. I was vulnerable too soon. I didn't call him enough. I called him too much. I didn't kiss him the right way. I smelled funny. I'm not pretty. I'm too fat. I'm too thin. I've got too many pimples on my face. I'm too forward. I'm too shy. I talk too much. I don't say the right things.* But if a man really liked me and let me have my way in our relationship, I became unattracted to him, thinking he was too weak minded, and quickly dumped him. I was constantly chasing the ideal man, only to find out the perfect man did not exist.

No matter who the guy was or what the situation, my self-deprecating monologues replayed themselves over and over. It was terrible. The mental gymnastics were exhausting. And it all stemmed from my deep-rooted feelings of rejection, insecurity, lack of identity, and mostly my strong desire to be loved.

In hindsight, I can see many times when all those failures with men were actually feeble attempts at fixing the broken relationship I had with my dad. If I could make a guy love me, that would make up for the fact that my dad didn't. I was trying to find the one who would fit perfectly into my empty heart. Of course that One could only be Jesus, but I didn't know that back then. I was determined to find a man, my dream man, to fill those shoes, even if I needed to sell my soul to do it.

———•———

It was a Friday night at Marshall's, a downtown club Kimmie and I frequented. Black leather couches and palm trees adorned the art deco–styled popular hangout, splashed by geometric patterns of bright reds and deep purples. Though we were underage, we knew the owner and he always let us in.

My dirty-blond hair defied gravity and stayed perfectly in place thanks to a shiny pink can of sticky Aqua Net hairspray. A Lycra top and miniskirt showed off my thin yet curvy shape. My best friend and I danced to the sounds of "Addicted to Love," tossing our heads back and wearing our signature seductive smiles that we flashed to the guys we liked, hoping to secure some free drinks—and we usually did. As we moved in rhythm, I noticed two tall, dark, and handsome men swagger into the club. One wore a silver fox fur coat, the other a black mink. Both sporting Gucci aviator sunglasses, they took long, deliberate strides toward the bar, checking out the mad scene of dancing bodies and overflowing drinks dripping sloppily onto the ash-covered floor. The men sat down, sunglasses still on, and slowly sipped on cognac.

Dollar signs flashed in my eyes. I grabbed my bestie. "Check out those dudes." Sunglasses or not, we knew they were watching us. We were young, hot, cocky. We knew the game well, at least this one. Sure enough, the guys beckoned us over, and we spent the next few hours throwing back drinks and swapping flirtations. They told us they were businessmen. (I know, vague, right?) Kimmie and I were impressed. It's easy to be when you're young and naive.

What we didn't know, and learned only after I moved to Las Vegas and was turned out (meaning being taught by a pimp or another prostitute how to sell myself), was that they were "circuit pimps," pimps who travel from city to city, finding and moving working girls (prostitutes) around. They had connections all over the United States and nice places to stay: mansions and high-rise condominiums. They lived the life, and it showed.

My friend hit it off with one of the guys. The other was not at all my type. He seemed too old for me. Before the night ended, she and I made a pit stop at the bathroom. As we teased our hair and swiped on more lipstick, I quipped, "Girl, they have money, and lots of it."

Kimmie started dating one of the guys. He lavished her with expensive gifts, namely this huge diamond rock I was convinced was fake and had probably been purchased at some cheap mall kiosk. I asked my friend to get it appraised. Imagine our shock when a reputable jeweler told us that it was worth between

$25,000 and $30,000! Not only was she sporting a blinding rock on her finger, she was also driving around in a flashy, custom-painted, pearl-white Mercedes-Benz, decked out in trim from the door handles to the rims in 24K gold. This wasn't the norm for a small-town girl who was used to going muddin' in pickup trucks. This was something new, a rich lifestyle that commanded my attention, and ultimately my worship.

A few weeks after they met, Kimmie and her new man took off for beautiful Hawaii. I stayed in freezing Minneapolis working three jobs for chump change. Oh sure, I had enough money to pay my bills and some nice clothes to impress guys at the club, but nothing that made a dent in my college fund, which at this point was pretty close to a big fat zero.

One day Kimmie called while I was on lunch break. "Annie," she said excitedly into the phone with a background cacophony of crashing waves. "I'm sitting on the beach talking on my own cell phone! Can you believe it? And I'm making, like, five hundred to one thousand–plus bucks an hour! You have got to come over here! I'll cover your plane ticket!" She told me what she was doing without actually saying it, which, simply put, was prostitution. The way she told it, it wasn't about selling your body. It was about the hustle of having the money given to you. "You don't have to actually have sex," she reassured me. "You can just get in the room, get the money, and run out. You won't believe how easy it really is!"

It didn't take a math genius to figure out the difference between the kind of cash she was making versus my measly $3.47 an hour. And it didn't take much for me to entertain the tempting offer. I was tired of being overworked and under-paid. At the time, I'd moved out of my sister's place and was sharing an apartment with a friend from work, and the rent wasn't cheap. So I traded in my long, black wool coat and snow boots for a neon-pink bikini and flew to Hawaii. I decided I'd spend some time with Kimmie and then go to Los Angeles for a few days to visit an ex-boyfriend who had been transferred from Minneapolis to California because of a military assignment. I just needed to see him again. I realized that he had my heart, and my heart wasn't willing to let go that easy.

As the plane inched closer to the Aloha State, I pressed my face against the window, transfixed by the crystal-clear aqua waters and the outline of the tropical green islands. I was so excited to be on a two-week vacation I could barely sit still. *Oh my gosh! This is really happening! I can't believe it!* What my friend was doing in Hawaii, and what she was encouraging me to do, didn't quite sink in. At least I didn't want it to at that moment.

When I stepped into Kimmie's hotel room, I admired the casual yet pricey decor, the artwork showcasing ornate conch shells and beach scenes, the elegant wicker furniture lost in a sea of stunning sundresses, strappy sandals, and multiple pairs of designer sunglasses. *Gosh, my friend has so many beautiful clothes!* I jumped on the plush bed, screaming at the top of my lungs, while Kimmie relaxed on an elegant chaise lounge and giggled at my excitement. We had made it! This place was awesome!

I immediately fell in love with the island, the life. Who wouldn't? It was Hawaii! It was breathtaking. In a sunlit haze, I strolled on the beach of the sapphire sea, inhaling the intoxicating scents of exotic flowers. Soothing melodies poured out of a ukulele played by a local while people in colorful bathing suits splashed in the ocean and other tanned bodies threw Frisbees. My feet dug into warm sand as the tropical breeze swept over my face. The gray skyscrapers of downtown Minneapolis and the freezing rain, snow, and whipping wind seemed a distant memory as the sun baked my skin a golden bronze on Waikiki Beach.

I got a fake ID within the first few days through a connection Kimmie had. I chose the name Fallen from the character Fallon on the hit TV show *Dynasty*. She was the most gorgeous woman I had ever seen. I wanted to be like her—smart, sophisticated, sexy . . . and *rich*!

Kimmie introduced me to the life of prostitution, but she didn't know what she was getting herself, or me, into. She looked at being a high-class call girl from the perspective of what she was gaining. Her boyfriend showered her with diamonds. He draped her in a designer wardrobe. He bought her a fancy car. So what if she turned a few tricks at night? During the day she was sipping a cocktail under sweeping palm trees and enjoying the perks of making insane money sometimes even just for performing the simple act of taking off her clothes. (Kimmie never considered her boyfriend a pimp because she believed he was completely in love with her.)

My friend didn't have to goad me into following her lead. After being groomed by the American dream, pop culture, Disney, music videos, romance novels, fashion magazines, night clubs, soap operas, you name it, I figured out pretty quickly that by being beautiful, I could get virtually anything I wanted.

Don't mistake me. I knew prostitution was wrong, but the temptation to pull in that much money in a few hours because someone desires you was too strong. As I listened to Kimmie talk endlessly about the cool stuff she had and how much fun she was having and how her boyfriend adored her and how he gave her anything she wanted, the intrigue overrode my whispering conscience. But more than that, because my heart had been so broken and I had been raped more times than I wanted to admit, a sense of apathy had set in.

I was numb, honestly, and I just didn't care anymore. Sure, I wanted to fall in love and live in the center of a fairy tale, but dark reality was quickly closing in around me to the point where I could barely see that Cinderella dream anymore. But I knew what I could see: Money. And lots of it. Fame. Success. And men I could use as a means to get those things. Heck, maybe I could buy my own real castle one day?

Prostitution was at its peak in Waikiki in the late eighties and early nineties. Japan's economy was booming, and many travelers from that area vacationed and bought property in Hawaii. I knew a thing or two about Japanese men. They were very respectful, kind, and gentle. Kimmie and I made a pact that we would only hit on the Japanese tourists for that reason. We didn't want to put ourselves in danger.

We got ready my first night there with beautifying precision. We looked classy, not like the stereotypical, dilapidated street-walker I had always envisioned. You know, the old and wrinkly kind with missing teeth and torn fishnets that you typically see in movies and television. Kimmie and I wore miniskirts that showed off our toned legs and lacy cropped tops underneath *Miami Vice*–style blazers. We made a pact to keep an eye on one another. We would only take "doubles," tricks where the two of us could stick together.

We hopped in Kimmie's bronze convertible Mustang as twilight danced on the horizon, the sky brushed soft with hints of pink, orange, and purple. We drove down to the congested Kalakaua Avenue, the main thoroughfare in Waikiki Strip. Japanese men littered the sidewalks like candy. Horns honked, neon signs blared, and traffic congested this tropical paradise. Kimmie showed me the "track" (a street where prostitutes walk up and down to pick up their dates) and taught me how to proposition men speaking Japanese. Her boyfriend's friend had taught her.

I set my sights on a good-looking Japanese man in his early forties and coyly sidled up to him. Staring deeply into his eyes and with a sexy slip of my blazer to show him what he could find underneath, I asked this man in his native tongue if he wanted to come with me and play. He said yes. My friend and I baited my trick's friend, and together we made our way to their nearby Hilton hotel. We blared our music and flirted with them as we sailed through green lights.

When we got to their room, it turned out that I didn't have to do a thing except perform my striptease act because that's all it took to arouse him, so I ended up making $500 in less than ten minutes. Prostituting myself for the first time filled me with an intense lust for money. It was a powerful drug. Like a scene from the *Lord of the Rings*, once I slipped on that ring of selling myself and the incredible money and influence that came with it, I couldn't take it off. This was going to be my secret way of making it in life—and no one would ever find out.

Turning tricks in Hawaii was pretty glamorous with the perfect combination of fancy hotels and sweet, rich men. The Japanese men were easy to control, and I had no reason to fear that they were going to turn into a maniac and kill me. Most nights Kimmie and I drove around looking for dates or walked up and down the track, inviting tricks (a.k.a. potential clients) back to our or their hotel room. We didn't have to do much work selling ourselves; the men were drawn to us like magnets. It was too easy!

I pocketed thousands of dollars during my stay. Not bad for a few nights, right? My friend and I hit the clubs after work, plunking down cash for high-end liquor drinks. During the day, we lay on the beach or wore out the soles of our shoes shopping at luxury boutiques.

I didn't think too deeply about what I was doing, selling my body for cash. It was easy to do because I was the sophisticated Fallen, not Annie. My alter ego was titanium, strong, unshakeable. Because of her, I was able to dissociate myself from what I was doing. Also, I enjoyed the power over these men that it seemed I had; it was a challenge and a rush to see if I could control them with my body and my looks. Plus I could think about the crazy money I was making and dream up plans to do something great with it instead of thinking about the fact that I was servicing strange men.

I also figured that if I had things like a nice house and a new car, I was going to attract success and a possible millionaire because of my independence and hefty bank account. What had hurt me in previous relationships was being dependent on someone I trusted. But I thought if I controlled the reins, well, I could finally have a say in my destiny.

After my two weeks in Hawaii, I headed off to Los Angeles to spend time with my ex. Before that, though, Kimmie's boyfriend decided to check out the Hollywood scene to see how lucrative prostitution was there. He made arrangements to fly to California with Kimmie and drive up and down the track on Sunset looking for tricks and then later hook up with a Beverly Hills escort service. I figured after getting my man fix from my military dreamboat, I could meet up with them and make some cash myself. My broken and bitter heart was possessed by greed and a lust for new adventures and excitement, an easy way to fill my empty places.

My ex drove me around Beverly Hills, where I saw my first Rolls-Royce and more sprawling mansions atop beautiful manicured lawns and swaying palm trees than I had ever seen, even on TV. We drove down the famous Rodeo Drive, where it seemed almost every woman was decked out in a pretty Chanel suit and carrying shopping bags from luxury boutiques. I was so naive and impressed!

The night Kimmie and I tested the waters, or rather the streets of Hollywood, we drove up and down Sunset Avenue in a rented car. The Boulevard featured endless rows of bars and clubs like the famous Roxy, Whiskey, and Rainbow. The sidewalks were packed with eighties hair band–looking dudes chugging beer and women with even bigger hair hanging on them dressed in tight, barely there clothing.

But the partying scene wasn't what caught my eye. I couldn't stop staring at the unusual number of tall, manly looking women wearing wild wigs and sporting so much makeup you couldn't see skin. As a small-town girl, they looked like something out of a movie. And even though they looked beautiful and wore high heels and sequined dresses and were draped with bold costume jewelry, they looked, well, masculine! There was no denying the Adam's apples or the distinct muscularity in their legs. Those were the first transvestite prostitutes Kimmie and I had ever seen. They walked the streets like they owned them. It was their town. Honestly, the whole vibe freaked us out, and we drove off toward our hotel, never once stepping out of our car. The Hollywood track wasn't what we thought it would be.

Kimmie's boyfriend told us he had a spot in Vegas and would take us there for a few days to make a little money. I had never been to Sin City before. Not only was I impressed that this dude had another house in another state, I was anxious to visit the popular destination I had only read about or seen on TV. The whole experience of traveling to new places was exhilarating. I could be whoever I wanted to be, just as I felt when moving so often as a child. I felt sophisticated, important, special—the lustful feelings that drove my empty heart.

The three of us hopped in a car for the four-hour drive. My heart beat faster the closer we got to the Vegas Strip. I was so excited. I rolled down my window, my face blasted by the warm, dry air. As we drove alongside camping trailers, tourist buses, sports cars, and limousines, I was transfixed by the bold, colorful signs of the many motels inviting you to play, eat, sleep, dream. The bigger resorts, like the original Sands and the Desert Inn, towered over palm trees that lined the sidewalks where tourists snapped pictures with bulky cameras. The city drew me in immediately with the hypnotic landscape of flashing neon lights and the beckoning energy of fun.

Kimmie hooked up with an escort agency while I "freelanced" or "walked the carpet" on my own. Instead of going on escort calls, I hung out at the bars in the casino, eyeing the men I could turn into a trick. My way, my hustle, my money.

I'll never forget wearing my father's royal-blue cardigan sweater my first night working in Las Vegas. I had taken it from his closet when I lived in Wisconsin, and though it was baggy,

I cinched it up with a wide sequined belt and wore a revealing lacey tank underneath. Sexy and chic.

I staked my claim at Caesar's Palace. Though the Vegas scene was mesmerizing—the flashing lights, the constant ringing of slot machines, the crowd of people standing shoulder to shoulder with jackpots gleaming in their eyes, the cocktail waitresses in their teeny skirts and busting bosoms balancing trays of drinks—I kept my excitement contained. I was still underage and couldn't gamble or drink. If any of the security guards got wind of how young I was, I could end up in jail. It's an artful balance, being seductively alluring to draw men your way while not attracting the wrong kind of attention.

I sat at the bar, below impressive chandeliers that gave off a soft light, and eyed the well-dressed crowd that started to gather around the sleek cocktail tables. A gentleman with salt-and-pepper hair in his late fifties sat down beside me. As he reached forward with his hand to get the bartender's attention, I noticed his gold Rolex watch. *Cha-ching!*

After he ordered a drink, he turned to me. I had discreetly moved my stool closer to his so he could catch a whiff of my expensive French perfume and so I could be close enough to lightly touch his arm if we were to chat.

He smiled at me, my open invitation.

"What are you doing here?" I asked in a flirtatious tone.

"I'm here on business," he answered. "Can I buy you a drink?"

While I nursed my rum and Coke, he asked what I was doing. "I'm here on business too. My name is Fallen, and I'm here to make men happy." I inched my way closer, placing my manicured hand on his forearm. "Do you want to go upstairs and get happy?"

The man turned bright red. I didn't let his embarrassment stop me and did my best to close the deal. "You can either spend your money on the floor and take your chances, or spend your money on me. Your best bet, of course, is to stick with me because I'm going to guarantee you a good time."

It was easy to turn on the charm, to activate Fallen. She could get practically any man into a bed. She was fearless, confident, and in charge. It didn't take long for us to make our way into his hotel room. A half hour later I left with $500 (with the rate of inflation that's just about $1,000 today). He stayed in bed with a smile.

I turned about ten tricks in a few days, pocketing more money than I knew what to do with. The day I flew back home to Minneapolis, I had already made my choice. I hugged my newly purchased Chanel purse close to my chest and tuned out the flight attendant reciting safety instructions. Peering out the window as the colors of Vegas dulled and white puffs of clouds surrounded the jet, I made an official plan to make my dreams come true. I'd keep my job at IDS but quit my moonlighting jobs at the Japanese steakhouse and pizza place, using those open slots in my schedule to work nights as a fancy high-class call girl. I thought about my love for music and dreamt about the guitars, keyboards, and sound equipment I could buy to help write my own music. I set my own footrace, seeing how fast I could make good money.

Vacation was over. When I went back to work after my two-week break, the microcosm of my world in Minneapolis hit me with shocking force. The frigid air whipped my face as I walked speedily through the parking deck, up the elevator, and resumed my duties working with microfiche and the IBM computer in my cubicle.

After my first day back, I pulled a giant yellow phone book out of my kitchen drawer and looked up escort agencies. I dialed the number of one at random and made arrangements to begin working. I was given a beeper and told they'd be in touch when calls came in.

My experience was nothing like prostituting myself in Hawaii. It wasn't as glamorous. Though I had some clients who lived in beautiful lakeside homes, there were times I found myself in seedy motel rooms and apartments that hadn't seen a mop or vacuum in years and that reeked of urine. I never felt safe being in that type of environment. And the money compared to Hawaii was terrible.

As hard as I tried to keep my new part-time job under wraps, some people caught on. My sister wasn't one of them, however. She was busy with work and life. We never spoke much about my personal life other than the guy I was into at the moment.

I was at work one day, combing through a ledger sheet for one of our clients, tapping my foot to the beats of Janet Jackson playing low on my mini pink boom box, when my supervisor buzzed in my line. "Annie." She sounded concerned. "Can you come into my office for a few minutes?"

My friend in the adjoining cubicle overheard her and mockingly joked, "Oooh, you're in trouble."

"Maybe I'm getting a raise," I retorted, laughing and putting aside my ledger. I did hear some rumbling in the office gossip chain that I was possibly being considered for a promotion into another department.

The minute I sat down in my supervisor's office, I knew something was wrong. I doubted this impromptu meeting had anything to do with getting a raise.

"Annie, I don't even know how to begin to say this." She nervously wrung her hands and looked down at her desk. When her eyes gazed back into mine, there was something about them, a sense of compassion. I still felt uncomfortable, but noticed a slight release of anxiety.

"Annie, I heard, um, a rumor that you were, uh, selling your body in Hawaii."

My heart raced like the speed of sound, and I shifted awkwardly in my seat. How on earth did she find out? I did tell a friend of mine at work, but surely she wouldn't betray my confidence. Would she? I was so embarrassed but denied every bit of the truth. The next day I resigned.

What a shame. What a waste! I was doing so well at IDS, and I was beginning to get noticed by the higher-ups and was being assigned more responsibilities. Looking back, I know I would have moved far up that corporate ladder into an executive position, but I foolishly tossed away all that potential for what I thought was my American dream of making money and being a successful businesswoman.

My supervisor wasn't the only one who called me out. I had made many friends hanging out at the clubs, namely local musicians, including the band Mazarati, formed by Prince. I never considered myself a groupie, although I dated several band members, including a few from Mazarati. I just wanted to do music. And that day came, when one of my friends in the Prince circle asked if I wanted to sing some background vocals for a friend on an album his friend was recording. *Yes, please!* I was in the studio one evening, the same one where Janet Jackson recorded her album *Control*, laying down vocal tracks for one of his buddies, when I got paged.

"I've got to go," I told my friend Eric. "I'll be right back." I grabbed my long wool coat off the chair and started walking toward the door, trying to remember where I had last seen the closest pay phone.

Eric reached out for my arm before I could leave and started giving me the third degree. "Whoa, wait a second. What do you mean? Where are you going? And why do you have a beeper?"

I rolled my eyes and tried to pull away, but he wouldn't let go. "Annie, what are you doing? Are you selling drugs?" he asked with genuine concern.

"No, uh, of course, uh, not . . ." I stammered, suddenly feeling guilty, ashamed.

"Oh, come on, Annie, what's going on?" He continued to hound me with question after question, and though at first I denied every one of his accusations, I finally burst into tears and told him the truth. "Look," I sputtered, the words falling out with force. "It's no big deal. I go on calls. I make good money. What are you in my grill for? Let it go!" The strange thing was, I wasn't really ashamed of what I was doing at the time; I just felt shamed when others knew my business.

He took me to dinner later that night, bringing with him a Gideon Bible. As my soup got cold, he read to me passages from the New Testament about Jesus and His love for people, for sinners. He read about Mary Magdalene, the woman at the well, the woman caught in adultery. "Annie, what you're doing is a terrible thing. You've got to stop it!" I didn't detect a tone of judgment from his words; it was clear Eric cared for my soul.

I felt bad. I really did. I cried, almost choking on the ice water I forced myself to drink, trying to get a grip. I agreed with him. He was right, I said. I had to stop selling my body. That night, through a heartfelt prayer to God, I decided to quit the escort business. I wouldn't sell my body ever again, no matter how tempting the money or the offer.

But I still needed to pay my bills, so I took up stripping instead. It seemed an obvious alternative. I loved music. I loved to dance. And I loved men. Besides, stripping to me wasn't the same thing as prostitution because I believed that if a man wasn't allowed to touch your body, you were just a visual fantasy and weren't getting paid for sex. (I now realize the absurdity of my thinking. Truth is, if a man is looking at you with a fantasy in his head, he is lusting after you, and more than likely will act on that lust through porn, self-gratification, or other women.) But, of course, I didn't think of those implications.

I got gigs through an entertainment agency called Party-Time that sent me to different clubs and bachelor parties and even to popular establishments in nearby Wisconsin. Stripping was not easy to do at first. I was scared to death, petrified at the thought of a group of men seeing my nearly naked body and dancing in skyscraping stiletto heels I could barely even walk on. Having two shots of tequila and listening to the pulsating music before I got on stage helped. Eventually it became easier. The attention was addicting. I started to love teasing guys who professed their undying love for me. I swayed on shiny poles on many a catwalk stage, enticing men with my slow gyrations while they threw tens and twenties at my feet. While I would flash customers to bring home a few extra bucks, I never did private lap dances or anything "extra." At least not at first.

Every club was different. Some were seedy, some more luxurious. But still, a strip club is a strip club, no matter how fancy it looks. All kinds of men frequented these "Gentleman's Cabarets"—young, old, married, single, blue collar, suits, you name it. As a stripper, I was a guy's ultimate fantasy. I could be whatever they wanted me to be, no strings attached.

One of the regular customers who stands out was a heavyset man we dancers nicknamed "Pete the Millionaire." Every time I danced, he forked over at least $400 at my feet. I took turns with the other girls dancing for Pete so everyone could get a piece of the action.

I worked hard, booking as many gigs as I could a day, keeping only a night or two free so I could do my own partying. After a while, I got a few regulars. I called them my fans. They would fill up every first row seat at the cocktail tables by the stage and toss the greenbacks my way, raising their sweaty brows in approval of my more risqué moves. Some of the guys seemed to be genuinely interested in me. Some of them even asked me why I was stripping. "Fallen, you're a smart girl," they'd tell me. "What are you doing in a place like this?" Fallen just smiled sweetly and thanked them for what I guessed was a compliment.

Stripping on a stage was far safer than meeting strange men at run-down motels. I felt secure in the strip joints, quite untouchable. But the thrill only lasted for a brief time. Some of the attention got creepy. A few guys got weirdly obsessed with me, hunting me down at the end of shows; some of them even proposed.

The hard fact is, just taking off your clothes on a stage, several feet away from groping hands, doesn't earn you a ton of money. A few months after I started stripping, my checking account was practically depleted. Looking at my bank statements made me depressed. I had bills and rent to pay. I was living on my own for the first time in a charming downtown apartment outfitted with black-and-gold lacquer furniture, satin couches, and music equipment I bought with my earnings, including an electric Fender Stratocaster guitar, a Korg M50 keyboard, and a Hohner guitar. It was expensive living on my own, and my life-style was definitely not cheap. I needed some cold, hard cash and fast. Pride kicked in. I couldn't lose my very own first place! That would make me look bad to others, especially after I quit my good job at IDS . . . it would embarrass me.

One of my regulars, a blue-collar average Joe who would follow me to all my local shows, had been asking me for weeks to hang out. Mind you, this wasn't to watch a movie and share a tub of popcorn. I finally gave in. He was a nice enough guy, and I felt safe around him. Why not let him pay me to have sex with him? My alter ego coaxed me, "Get on with yourself, Annie. Step aside so Fallen can get this money—she will handle everything just fine."

So I resorted to the quick fix, the easy way out, the path of the familiar. Sleeping with that one client set me on a down-ward spiral, but at this point in my life I didn't care anymore. I knew I'd do this over and over, but it was my decision and I figured I could quit whenever I wanted to. The truth is, greed took over my heart.

I started taking more and more clients up on their offer to pay good money for a quickie in their hotel or at their home.

The money poured in slowly and sporadically. I had a good thing going, or so I thought. Annie had started to fade away at this point. The egomaniac Fallen fed my thoughts, convincing me this was what I needed to do: I was smart, learning how to use what I had to earn a bankroll, and ultimately it was a win-win if I could make a lot of money to justify the means.

I had the power. I had the control. But when you keep playing with matches, it's only a matter of time before a tiny spark ignites a roaring, uncontrollable fire that destroys everything around you.

CHAPTER 3

HE WHO SOLD ME A DREAM

"Much dreaming and many words are meaningless."
—Ecclesiastes 5:7 NIV

The Skyway Lounge in downtown Minneapolis was a happening strip joint. Slick businessmen in fancy suits strolled in for lunch and after work, ties loosened, money rolling. The tips were great, the best in the area, and dancers lined up to work at this place. I was lucky to be a regular.

One Saturday night I was dancing to Prince's "Kiss," giving some special customers a little extra glimpse of skin, when in walked a man who caught my attention. The bright lights illuminating the catwalk stage couldn't distract me from how gorgeous he was. A cross between a young Billy Dee Williams and Denzel Washington, he wore a gray tweed suit and pointy loafers. He walked confidently, light and smooth, his Jheri curl pulled back in a sleek ponytail.

Mr. Hotness moved toward the stage, almost in rhythm to the blaring song, and sat down in front of me. He looked up at my face and, never taking his eyes away for a second, pulled out a couple of twenties and laid them before me like a five-course meal for a starving girl.

I was so taken aback by how good-looking this guy was and the obvious attention he was giving me, I almost tripped over my stilettos. I was so nervous, he might as well have been my first schoolgirl crush. The tip he left was big, and I owed him some well-earned attention in return. So I finished the rest of my set in his honor, dancing just for him.

The song ended, and to the tune of echoing applause and catcalls, I walked up the spiral staircase to the dark but spacious dressing room. Bright bulbs outlined the wall-length mirror. Counter space overflowed with bottles of lotion, glitter, hair spray, countless tubes of mascara and lipstick, and empty beer bottles and shot glasses smeared with faint lipstick marks. Clothing racks rammed in the corner were stuffed with revealing, sparkly outfits; puffy feather boas and stripper shoes in all sizes littered the floor. I stared in the mirror and did a final beauty check. Anxiously fixing my tousled hair, I wondered if that heavenly vision of a man was still downstairs. Maybe he'd even talk to me. I was giddy with excitement. Ah, the wonders of lust.

When I walked into the main area of the strip club, sashaying through the smoky haze as cool as I could be, I smiled and made sweet small talk with some of my regulars but politely refused their offers for a drink. Turned out the man I was interested in was waiting for me at the bar.

"I'm Julian," he said, offering a warm, lingering handshake. "And you, baby, are super fine! My kind of woman!"

I blushed shyly at the compliment. "I'm Fallen." My nerves got the best of me, and the pitch of my voice embarrassingly shot up a seeming octave higher.

We talked for a bit, him twirling the drink in his hand in slow, deliberate circles. Julian told me he was a businessman. I never asked for specifics. I imagined he was successful, whatever his work, by the look of his shiny gold watch, which was dripping with diamonds. Julian was extremely charming, sweet, and smart. I was impressed. And I liked him. A lot. Too much, in fact. Something deep inside me said this man and my desperate desire for him was dangerous, but my fantasy of what the relationship could be far outweighed my reasoning. This could be "the one," the love of my life.

Drinks turned into dinner later that night outside the club. More talking, more flirting, more desperate desire. Even though I had many relationships that tore my heart in two, I wasn't willing to give up that easily. Though I desired both love and money, money had proven to be a more reliable companion—but if love became part of the package, great! With Julian I felt there was a heated spark of hope left. I believed I had a soul mate out there somewhere, and I was determined to be happy in love, no matter the cost. I was suspicious of men, which is why it was easy for me to get money out of guys in the strip club, but I still wore my heart on my sleeve. Julian was no dummy. He saw right through me from the start—a teenage girl, broken but desperately craving attention.

We started dating immediately. The romance was swift, but I didn't care because I wanted to dive right in. Julian, who was a few years older, took me shopping frequently. He'd buy me sexy dresses for the clubs and ornate yet skimpy costumes for my shows. He'd surprise me with gold necklaces and diamond earrings and tell me, "Baby, I want to give you this because you're very special to me." I'll admit, I loved being spoiled. I was just as materialistic as he was. We were the perfect match in that respect. I wanted him to be wealthy and make money so he could spend it on me.

Julian was an awesome dancer, and we spent many nights shaking our booties at the local nightclubs. He was well known by many of the Minneapolis club and bar owners, and many of them would let us in without having to pay the cover charge. That impressed me! We would roll right into the VIP sections where the big boys of the city sprawled out over leather couches, enjoying the overt, adoring attention of beautiful young ladies.

My man was a romantic, always buying me single red roses and singing in my ear. He'd get real close, nuzzle my neck, and sweetly sing classic R&B love songs like, "You Are My Lady" by Freddie Jackson: "You are my lady / You're everything I need and more . . ." He reeled me in with these songs, caused my heart to go pitter-patter, and made me feel as though I was on top of the world.

We'd take long rides in his brand-new Lincoln Continental, talking about our dreams, the things we would do together. He'd say, "Baby, I know you want more out of life. I do too. We have so much in common!" At this point I didn't even question what he did for a living, or the cash he always seemed to have on hand. Everything he said fit perfectly with what I thought I wanted for my life. Though I was head over heels in love, I kept our passionate romance quiet, just like I did my escort jobs. Besides, no one would understand the love and desire I had for this guy.

Whenever we went out, Julian held me close, proudly displaying me as "his woman." I liked that. One night his possessive side showed its true colors. We were at a club when some random guy grabbed my butt while I was getting us some drinks. I whipped around and gave the guy a dirty look and marched, shots in hand, right up to Julian. I told him what had happened and he went wild. Julian erupted in a rage, eyes wild with fire, and roared, "Where is he? Where's that guy?" as he maniacally looked around the dance floor for the unsuspecting dude. When I pointed him out, Julian got in his face, screaming obscenities, and punched him right in the mouth, knocking out the guy's two front teeth. Fellow clubbers circled around like vultures while Julian pounded balled-up fists into the guy's face. Someone called the police, who swiftly arrived on the scene and hauled my man to jail. Julian was in cuffs, getting dragged out of the club by men in uniform, when he yelled, "I love you, baby!" I felt protected. Julian was my prince, my guardian, my hero, and I was his princess. Just as I had always dreamed about.

I quickly grew to trust Julian. One day we were lying on my black satin couch watching a movie when he turned to me and asked where I was getting the money to afford all this nice stuff—the clothes, the music equipment, the designer handbags. "Dancers aren't true hustlers to the bone," he casually remarked, "they just think they are. But they really don't know how to make a lot of money."

I laughed and proudly puffed out my chest. "Well, I do!"

Julian leaned in closer, his fingers seductively trailing down the side of my face. "Oh really? How's that?"

I had no reason to lie. I didn't see the need. I felt comfortable with him, open. I bragged that every client in the strip club was a john (a.k.a. "tricks" or "dates") to be tricked. How naïve the men I met were. I didn't want him thinking I was a whore, however, and made it clear that the only reason I was doing this was to save up money for college. I was a smart businesswoman. Escorting was a temporary fling. I also made sure to point out I wasn't doing it all the time.

I expected some sort of shock, or at the least an expression of surprise, but Julian simply nodded, as if having sex with strangers for money were a natural side job. "Wow," he said, nodding with approval. "That's hip, baby. I dig it. Good for you! I got me a hustling woman!"

I'm sure he already knew what I was doing before I told him. Like I said, he wasn't stupid. Julian made another strange comment during our conversation. He mentioned something about me bringing in more money than his other squares. I didn't take Julian's nonchalance and the odd remark as warning signs, however. I didn't think it strange that he didn't care I was sleeping with other men. In my mind, his acceptance of my part-time job only affirmed his love for me. *He gets it,* I thought. *And he loves me unconditionally. Jackpot, baby!*

I wasn't the only one with some secrets. Julian shared some with me, but not everything. He confided that he spent the last seven years in prison, selling me a dramatic sob story of how he had been set up by his ex-girlfriend, who worked in a massage parlor. According to him, she had lied to the police about some illicit activity he was involved with and as a result got wrongfully locked up in the penitentiary. Julian put on a convincing show of being the victim. He was trying to do the right thing in life but kept running into some bad luck. (I found out the truth when I moved to Vegas. He went to prison for attempting to set his ex's massage parlor on fire.)

He also admitted he dealt cocaine on the side, but I wasn't surprised. Crack cocaine was at its height in the late eighties, although I'd never done hard drugs before—just smoked pot occasionally. I was impressed with his opportunistic nature, his wisdom in taking advantage of the market. While I knew he was smart, I wasn't impressed with the possibility that he could get caught and go to jail for a long time. I tried to encourage him to stop. Time and time again I told him, "Look, we both have to figure out a new trade." We even talked about opening a jewelry store one day. It seemed like a good career move. I mean, I did love diamonds, precious gems, and gold.

Because I was curious why we never hung out at his place, he also told me he was living with a woman, who also happened to be a major dope dealer. "We're just friends," he promised, and reassured me nothing romantic was going on between them. Even though he said they were "just friends," I was extremely jealous of his time away from me.

The more I got to know Julian, the more I learned about his past. It wasn't pretty. He grew up on the streets and learned to survive by shooting dice. His dad left him when he was just a few years old. His mother hated Julian simply because he looked like his dad. Out of disgust, she would beat him mercilessly. When Julian was in his early teens, she finally told him, "I can't stand looking at you anymore. Get out!" He hit the streets on his own, not even a legal adult. I felt sorry for him, for the little boy in him who didn't even stand a chance. In hindsight, I can see where Julian's rage came from—his deep-seated anger not only toward his mother but also for a father he never knew.

Knowing his history made it a lot easier to turn a blind eye to his bad behavior and make excuses for him. And ignore the obvious. Our relationship was a ticking bomb, but I didn't see red flags. I only saw a man who needed love and a second chance at happiness. I understood that and could relate on some level to his pain. It drew me closer to him.

Dating Julian was hard, not just because of his past, but also because of the emotional intensity. There were no moments of calm. Everything about our relationship was heightened—our passion, our fights, our words, our desire, our emotions. If he didn't call one evening, I'd be devastated, spending the rest of the night with my stomach in knots, unable to sleep. When I wasn't with Julian, I actually felt sick, a familiar feeling I had with other boyfriends, including Jake. I was lovesick. I felt like I had no power over his overwhelming hold and all the emotions I was experiencing. I thought Julian was the cure for my sickness, and believe me, he knew it.

I would also compare my relationship with Julian to Kimmie's with her boyfriend. I admired how well he treated her. He was so warm and kind and often showered her with gifts. She felt adored, valued, fulfilled; I wanted to feel the same way. My love tank had been empty for so long, and I was desperate for attention—any attention, positive or negative—I devoured every word, every touch, and every false promise Julian threw my way. Toxic? Yes. Unhealthy? Definitely. But to me at the time? Nothing but true love! I saw Julian as the savior I had been waiting for my whole life. What I really needed was Jesus my Savior. Unfortunately I was so lost in this relationship that I was blind to the truth.

A few months after we started dating, sometime during the summer of 1988, Julian started standing me up. I'd page him but he wouldn't call back for hours, sometimes even days. One particular time we had made plans to have dinner and check out a club that had just opened. I waited for him at home, touching up my hair and makeup for the hundredth time, when I realized he wasn't coming. I was so angry. A few hours later, when he called to apologize and asked me to meet him somewhere, I told him I was done with the mind games. "It's over," I said. Even though in my heart, I didn't mean it—I knew that if I said it was over, it would hurt him and I could get even somehow. I was fed up with his behavior. As hard as it was to be apart, the roller-coaster ride of emotions was getting old. And I could no longer handle him not showing up for me on a regular basis. I needed to show him that I refused to be treated like a doormat.

That night I decided to check out the new club anyway with my girlfriend. I picked her up, venting the entire way about my jerk of an ex-boyfriend. How I was teaching him a lesson. I was running low on gas so I made a pit stop. As I held the nozzle in my hand, still steaming mad, my girlfriend piped up from inside the car, "Girl, you'll forget all about that dude once we get our drink on tonight! Pick yourself up another guy!"

I looked up at the sky, the twinkling bright lights gazing down on me, and sighed. I missed Julian, but maybe breaking up was for the best. In the middle of my silent monologue, I heard the sound of screeching tires and smelled rubber. I reoriented myself in just enough time to see Julian's car flying into the gas station. The tires squealed and the car came to a screeching halt, just inches away from hitting the back of my car.

I was stunned. I couldn't move. He jumped out of the car like an Olympian, the slamming door echoing in the quiet Minneapolis neighborhood, and started yelling obscenities at me. Before I could say a word, he pushed me against the metal car door, grabbed me by the neck, and gripped tight. And tighter. Until I realized I couldn't breathe. I blindly started swinging my hands at his face as my friend was screaming for help. All I saw was his fist. I crumpled to the ground, tearing my new miniskirt on the edge of the car door. I didn't know it at the time, but the minute I hit the concrete, he turned on my friend and started choking her and telling her to shut up. She Maced him! Then he was gone, with the same screech of tires fading into the distance.

(Side note: My friend who was with me that night recently reminded me of this incident as I was writing this chapter. I had completely put the entire episode out of my mind, I think out of denial. I didn't want to believe the man I loved was bad. She even showed me the pictures she took of me after Julian had hit me.)

My friend and I went to the police station that night and I filed a report. I stayed away from Julian for about a month, ignoring his phone calls and avoiding him at all costs. He left message after message apologizing, and he even showed up at one of the clubs where I danced. Every apology, every plea for mercy, included one or more or all of the following, laced with profanities where he deemed appropriate:

"I'm sorry I lost my temper."

"I don't know what got into me."

"I'll change."

"I can't live without you."

"You're *my* woman!"

"I don't want us to be apart."

"You make me go crazy!

"You're the best woman I've ever had!"

"I've never loved anyone as much as you!"

One evening I sat on the edge of a bed in a luxury downtown hotel watching a man count out loud a few hundreds that he slapped down on the marble dresser top. "Ready?" He smiled at me, putting out the cigarette that had accidently dropped ashes all over the plush carpet in his excited anticipation. Dialing up Fallen, I nodded seductively and beckoned him over. When he left twenty minutes later, leaving me to lie alone on the Egyptian cotton sheets for the rest of the forty minutes of the paid room, I thought about Julian.

Traveling back to my childhood, I remembered the scenes where my father begged my mom for forgiveness. She always accepted his tearful apologies. She forgave; I should too. In my heart I believed Julian's violent episode was an isolated incident. I thought of different reasons why his outrage would perhaps be justified. *Maybe he was set off by a childhood memory. Maybe someone did something to piss him off. Maybe he got conned out of a drug deal and lost money. Everyone deserves another chance. I mean, we all lose it from time to time, right?*

I missed him. How do you explain loving someone you fear? I don't know. It was the beginning of intense brainwashing, and also of me wanting to fix whatever was wrong with him and with us. I believed in the power of love so strongly that I was convinced it would change him and nothing like this would ever happen again. He was my beast, I was determined to be his beauty.

Julian and I got back together, and I even offered to let him move in with me. He had been talking about the problems he was having with his roommate, so it seemed a natural next step to get out of that messy situation and shack up with me. Recently I had moved into a brand-new apartment near the Lake of the Isles in a prestigious area of town. Beautiful custom mini mansions overlooked the tranquil waters near my complex. I felt like I had arrived. My apartment was small but stunning, with new appliances, sparkling tile, beautiful gold carpet, and shiny hardwood floors.

When Julian moved in with me, he brought with him a TV camera monitoring system that was connected to the Minneapolis probation department. Initially I didn't understand what the mesh of wires and equipment were about. I just thought it had something to do with the cable, VHS, or a gaming system. But when I saw the grainy black-and-white video footage of the police department, I was shocked. As Julian kneeled in front of the electronic gadget, turning knobs and adjusting settings, I demanded he tell me what was going on.

He added to the sob story he had told me earlier. As part of his probation, he was put on house arrest after serving time and wasn't allowed to leave the state. Each morning and night he had to check in with his probation officer via video camera.

I loved Julian deeply and felt he'd been cheated by life, by his ex, by the police. I wanted to be there for him, and I was, even though there were countless times he would disappear for hours before making sure to "check in" with the probation department on the camera. I always asked where he was. His typical response was that he was "taking care of business."

Over the next few months, the police started harassing Julian more frequently. He told me they were always on his tail, following his every move and frequently pulling him over on the road, giving him the third degree. In a way, I felt the cops were being prejudiced and were only messing with him because he was a black man dating a white chick. But things had to change. There was too much drama happening with the cops. I thought about moving. Besides, I was getting really tired of the exotic dancing scene in Minnesota, and Julian knew it.

So I made a drastic move. My girlfriend Kimmie had moved from Hawaii to Vegas. I called and asked her if Julian and I could visit for a few months, while still keeping our apartment in Minneapolis. Kimmie warned me Julian was up to no good and word on the street was that he was a violent man with a crazy temper, but I refused to believe her because I was in love. Believing her would wreck the fantasy I was in, as well as the potential for happiness I'd never known, so I assured her, "You don't know anything about him. He is sweet and kind and has a big heart."

Reluctantly, she agreed. Julian and I started packing up a few things, making plans to stay with Kimmie and her man for a week or two until we got settled on our own. I was so done with the Midwest. I wanted way more than this cold and dreary place had to offer. The lights were calling me home.

CHAPTER 4

BROKEN WINGS

"Unjustified ambition kills value,
Kills someone else's desire to fly."
—Dejan Stojanovic

We arrived in Las Vegas toward the end of 1988. Blasting "My Prerogative" by Bobby Brown, Julian and I drove down the desert highway as the sun lazily set over the horizon. Stretched-out clouds ablaze in purple and pink drifted over the muted sky, paving the way for the infamous scene of neon flashing lights. I leaned into my man, snuggling into his open arm, and sighed. Vegas was going to change my life. I just knew it.

My girlfriend and her boyfriend lived a few miles away from the Strip. We pulled into the driveway, parking next to her beautiful drop-top, custom-painted pearl white Benz, which looked oddly out of place in the modest neighborhood.

It was so good to see Kimmie, and we caught up over a few drinks. We chatted away on black, buttery leather couches that overlooked her swanky bar. My friend couldn't stop gushing over her man and how well he was treating her. She even showed me her most recent gift, a new cell phone. The gray, brick-sized monstrosity could barely fit in her purse. *Wow!* I thought. Except for in the movies, it was the first time I had ever seen a cell phone that wasn't connected to a car. When Kimmie gave me a tour of her pad and walked me into her bedroom walk-in closet, my mouth dropped to the floor. Beside the fact that it was twice the size of my apartment bathroom, it was stacked with high-end clothing. Endless rows of shoes lined one side, while on the other, Fendi, Chanel, and Louis Vuitton bags were meticulously hung in their glory. Kimmie had shoes and purses in every color imaginable and racks of dresses with the tags still on them. It was like standing in the middle of a *Vogue* magazine.

The next day Kimmie accompanied me to the escort service, the agency that would send me on my calls almost every day for the next five years. She coached me beforehand, warning me to make sure I told them I was a dancer/entertainer only— and not a prostitute. Prostitution was illegal in Las Vegas, and they didn't hire people who admittedly sold sex for money. Of course this was a cover-up to prevent them from getting shut down by vice, but I didn't need to let on that I knew it. Following my friend's directions, I sat down in front of a middle-aged woman who made copies of my Minnesota driver's license and laid out the ground rules for me. The process was cut and dry, impersonal and uncomfortable. Before I left, the woman at the agency gave me a beeper. I was disappointed. I had hoped I would get my first cell phone.

The arrangements, financial and otherwise, were clear. The agency received a flat fee of $150 for up to one hour of service for every call that came in. I was also informed that I would be fined $1,500 a night if I didn't follow my set schedule. (By the time I left the agency, I would owe them over $65,000! This is called debt bondage.)

Clients would call the agency and operators, or "phone girls," would match them with the appropriate working girl, a barely eighteen busty blonde, a slim and tan brunette college girl, an Asian beauty, a racy redhead housewife, and so on. In turn, the girls would tip the operator at least $50 or more per call. The bigger the tip, the better the calls she would send your way. What I charged for my particular services, well, that was up to me once I arrived.

Setting high expectations for myself right off the bat, I decided I was going to demand top dollar for my time. I wasn't a street hooker or a cheap date. I was Fallen, the sophisticated, classy escort. In my mind, I set a fee of five hundred to a thousand dollars (in addition to the agency fee) to simply start the party with minimal services like a massage. Any other type of sexual service cost more for up to an hour. At the current rate of inflation, my minimal fee would be no less than a thousand dollars today. And if the customer wanted another hour, that was double the agency fee and double my rate. At the end of my "shift," I'd return to the agency and give them the drop (the agency fees and tips for the operator). The rest was mine to keep. Jackpot!

I was an easy sell because I looked so young. The agency's phone was ringing off the hook with requests for "hot young blonde, barely eighteen." I got booked on four calls that first night. I was ready, decked out in an elegant and stunning white suit with a pencil skirt, white sky-high heels, and a white Chanel pintuck purse. Three of the calls were a no-go. One guy didn't show up at the hotel. The second wasn't at his house. The third didn't have the money.

My fourth and final call was at the Golden Nugget. I knocked on the door of a room in the lavish and ornate hotel. The quiet and empty hallway, lined with burgundy carpet and glistening gold light fixtures, was a stark contrast to the bustling energy of the casino and its nonstop ringing and spinning of slot machines and the pitter-patter of dealers running the card tables only a few floors down. A well-dressed man in his late sixties answered. Sweet and grandfatherly, he paid me $800 for roughly ten minutes. I had made more money than I ever brought in with a few nights of stripping.

I couldn't wait to tell Julian. He was going to be so proud of me! Kimmie and I met back up in the lobby in the early hours of the morning, as a now-sparse crowd of bleary-eyed people, young and old and likely with almost-empty pockets, continued to place bets and play the slots. Kimmie, who knew her way around the Vegas block, made more than I did, but she commented I did great for my first night. I could barely contain my excitement. I hadn't slept in over twenty-four hours but was wide-awake, running on high from the adrenaline of making so much money my first night in this gambling and party mecca.

The Strip was calm as we made our way home. The sun shone as yawning tourists headed to the famous breakfast buffets. We purred down the street in her sports car. I feasted on the sights of more hotels and casinos than I had ever seen.

When we walked in the door, our boyfriends were watching TV on the black leather couch. Clicking her heels on the white tiled floor, Kimmie excitedly blurted out to Julian, "Fallen did great! She made some good money tonight!"

Julian cocked his head to the side and nodded slowly. I didn't recognize the weird look on his face, but that thought was fleeting. Proud as a peacock, wide-eyed, and with cash in hand, I walked toward my man. "That's right!" I said.

And before I knew it, my few minutes of celebration came to an abrupt, violent stop. I wrote about this briefly at the beginning of the book, but here's the complete story:

"Give me your purse," Julian roared. He jumped up from the couch and reached out for my leather purse strap, practically knocking me over in the process.

"Whoa, whoa . . ." I stammered and took a step back, trying to regain my balance. I started walking into the kitchen to get some space. Julian followed right on my heels while my girlfriend and her man quietly watched the scene unravel from the corner of the living room.

"Break yourself!" he yelled even louder, cussing me out and calling me all kinds of vile names.

I knew what he meant. Bits and pieces of past conversations started fitting together into a grim puzzle. Back in Minneapolis, I had heard some talk from his friends about breaking yourself. It was an act of submitting to a pimp and turning over your prostitution earnings, officially becoming one of his girls. I remember many times rocking out to Too $hort's song "Don't Fight the Feeling," a rap duet about a pimp trying to break his girl. On one hand, I was offended by the artist's harsh and derogatory language, but on the other hand, I enjoyed the girl's comeback in the song, basically telling the pimp to hit the road (and I'm using very tame language here). I related to the woman in the song—there was no way I would ever have a pimp. Fallen was independent, and she commanded control of all she earned as an escort. I was completely against it!

So when Julian told me to break myself, I was outraged. *What is he thinking? Who does he think he is? I will never pay a pimp. This is my money!* I got right in his face and sassed him, "I'm not breaking anything. I earned this money. It belongs to me!"

As soon as the words flew out of my mouth, I was doomed.

Julian's face twisted in an evil contortion of rage. He grabbed me by the throat and slammed my entire body into a cupboard. I saw stars and blacked out while he grabbed a fistful of my long blond hair and dragged me to the back porch, my pretty white suit accumulating dirt and dust from the wild ride. He threw my thin body down on the cement. I faced the Vegas sky while Julian pounded away, punching me in the face and kicking my ribs. I heard the cracking of my bones as each blow fell hard and fast.

As he raged, my bloody body a lifeless punching bag, I weakly cried out, "Stop it! Oh, stop, please, please, just stop hitting me! I'll do what you want! You can have the money, please!" My words fell on deaf ears.

In the background, I heard Kimmie screaming at Julian to stop and threatening to call the police. Her boyfriend/pimp started yelling just as loud and locked her in her bedroom so she couldn't help me.

Julian flipped my body over and grabbed the back of my neck, his grip so tight my skin stayed bruised for weeks. He dragged me a few yards deeper into the yard where I could not mistake the crude stench of dog feces. The smell of wet grass suddenly turned putrid as Julian shoved my face into the fresh poop. I wanted to scream, but I knew what would happen if I opened my mouth. I could taste blood, even some pieces of teeth he had chipped, but there was no way I was going to have feces in my mouth.

My mind swirled with thoughts as I drifted in and out of consciousness. *Who is this man? I don't know him! This isn't Julian. This is a monster. Why is he beating me? Surely this is some mistake. Any moment now he's going to stop and say he's sorry.*

Julian bent down. I could hear him panting, drawing in quick breaths that were starting to slow down. "Get up!" he growled. Who was he kidding? I could barely move. I tried to roll to the side and cried out in pain. It hurt to simply breathe. My sight was blurred with blood, and as I slowly lifted my hand, wet and sopped in dog poop, to clear my eyes, I could feel tiny welts all over my head from his punches.

I tried to sit up and fell back down. Julian shook his head, and still kneeling over me, started screaming in my face that I was "out of pocket" (or out of line) and I needed to learn the rules of the game. As I moaned, he ranted, "You're lucky to be with me, let alone be alive! I won't be tolerating any disrespectful attitude! Look what you made me do to you because of your smart mouth! You're going to make me go crazy! I love you! I would die for you! I can't believe you were so disrespectful in front of our friends. Wipe them tears off your face and shut up before I take you out to the desert and bury you six feet under. This is *pimpin'*. Imma be your boss from now on!"

I heard every word he said, but it couldn't have been real. *It must be a dream*, I thought, groggy from the beating, *or a scene from a movie I watched the other day.* (Keep in mind that I have cleaned up Julian's language immensely. You cannot imagine how verbally abusive he was to me on top of all the physical pain he inflicted.)

Julian continued to scream as I closed my eyes and tried to wish away reality. "We can do this the easy way or the hard way, you decide. You either get with the program and get busy stackin', or I'll have you wish you had never been born! Stop that whimpering, don't be so weak! A real pimp needs a down woman, and I thought you were her. You need to prove me wrong! I can replace you with another girl and fly her down here from Minnesota. Is that what you want, huh? Huh?! Keep acting up and that's what I'll do!"

Right before I blacked out he said, "You'd better straighten up and realize what time it is." I don't remember much else except waking up in Kimmie's guest bedroom.

I opened my eyes hours later in the pitch-black darkness, sometime in the middle of the night. My head was pounding, my body ached. I was disoriented for a few minutes, not recognizing where I was. As I turned to the nightstand, I saw a framed picture of Kimmie and her boyfriend/pimp, their arms around each other. Then I remembered. I looked down at my naked body. My skin was a mess of dried blood, black bruises, and red welts. I tried to move but couldn't get out of the wet sheet I had perspired through. I groaned, and the tears flooded. Julian came into the room to make sure I didn't leave. I think he was scared I'd run—not like I could even if I tried—but didn't want to show it.

I felt sick to my stomach, from the physical pain and from the heartbreak. I couldn't believe someone who professed to love me could put his hands on me like that. I felt trapped. I wanted to escape, to run out the front door, but I couldn't even inch my way to the edge of the bed.

A pimp basically breaks you first by brainwashing you. He makes you dependent on him not only physically but emotionally. He makes you feel that you cannot possibly live without him, and if you try to, your life will have no meaning. He is your universe. He is your meaning. As soon as you start believing this, he's got you. And then, to solidify this control, he wraps up the deal by beating you into permanent submission. By then it's too late. You already love him. You won't leave, and he knows it. So he uses that love as a weapon to make you his slave. You become frozen. Afraid to rock the boat. Afraid to stand up and leave.

I was quiet while Julian sat beside me. I couldn't say a word. I couldn't even face him. When I finally did turn his way, I noticed he was gentle, calm, like the old Julian I knew. But I was scared. I couldn't trust him. Then he did something that blew my mind. He started crying. As his eyes filled with tears and he softly caressed my wet face with his finger, he started the inevitable apology.

"I'm so sorry I hurt you, baby. I really didn't mean to hit you. But you made me do it! Why did you question me? Baby, don't you see, I really do love you, but you having control of this money is not what the game is about. It's about trust. You're going to have to trust me with the bankroll. I'm a businessman, and I know what we are going to have to do with this cash to make it. You and me are like Bonnie and Clyde, and we need to be a strong team that's united. I'm going to buy you the clothes you never had growing up. You're going to get your dream car and do your music school like you want. You must understand why you can't ever disrespect me again, baby. You are a smart girl, and I know you are gonna be a star in this town. I love you, Fallen, my white woman!"

I lay in the bed in silence. My throat was parched, and I didn't even know how to respond. I simply nodded. He actually had the nerve to start dressing my wounds and bring me an icepack for my eye that was swollen shut. He put both of his arms around me as I lay there, helpless and afraid. I was shocked, still scared to death to even look directly in his eyes.

Julian took me to a hotel that morning. He didn't say a word to Kimmie or her boyfriend when we left. My friend pleaded with me to stay. "Don't go with him," she begged. She was frightened for my life, and rightfully so. I kept my head down and mumbled, "I'm sorry" as I inched my way out the front door, following Julian's lead.

Kimmie's boyfriend was on Julian's side because he was a pimp too. The pimp culture follows its own twisted ritual code of conduct—they have each other's back so they can keep things like this hush-hush. This was like a pat on the back from pimp to pimp, a symbol of their solidarity to one another and a reminder to other girls of who was in charge.

The beating I took and my willingness to stay with him changed my relationship with Kimmie. We would never be as close as we had been until years later.

———— • ————

That night in Las Vegas ended my naivety to the game. I thought it was all about me up until this time—having fun and making a lot of money—but now I realized the shocking truth about this game of power, lust, control, manipulation, and greed. Julian was my pimp now. He had broken me and put the fear of the beating in me . . . but also the fear of losing him as my lover. It also set the tone for the rest of our relationship, which would last for about five years. In essence, if I obeyed Julian and did what he said, he would never need to punish me like that. Although I still didn't want a way out of escorting, I did start planning how I would eventually leave Julian. I knew that I needed to get smart and stash money to make my escape.

Julian hovered over me for days, making sure I didn't go anywhere or call the cops. There was no way I could escape. I lay in bed in some random hotel I can't even remember for a few weeks before I could start working again. My ribs needed time to heal. While the bruises would eventually disappear, the pain in my heart would never go away.

A week or two after the beating, he bought me a Louis Vuitton handbag and a gold and diamond ring, showering me with compliments of how I was his woman and he was going to take care of me. He sat in bed with me, tending to my wounds while talking about how he understood pain because he didn't have a fair shake in life. He brought up the times his mother had beaten him. I sat and listened, my bruises and the memory of that night slowly fading. I felt so bad—for him.

I didn't hate Julian, even after he beat the living daylights out of me. Oh, I was scared of him and the potential he had to turn into a violent monster, but I loved him. Still. This is the part that is so hard for most people to understand.

Even I cannot believe now that I stayed with Julian for so long, but since I couldn't see past my situation, I remained committed to him out of love, but also out of terrifying fear: I feared losing my life or getting a beatdown that would disfigure me. I feared

I wasn't good enough for anyone to love, feared that Julian would come after my friends or family to find me if I ran away. He constantly threatened me, and he had a gun that he used to hold to my head while telling me he should shoot me, because if he couldn't have me, then nobody could.

I loved my man and was completely blind to the truth. Julian had many moments of being sweet, kind, and compassionate, reminding me that we were working for a better life, that we would get out of this game one day and do something that mattered. He sold me a dream, convincing me that life would be different. One day. I believed him. I had to. It's all I had.

That first major beating should have been my reality check, should have been proof that Julian and I would never have a fairy-tale-come-true relationship. But my self-esteem was gone. Julian had become my life. I believed the lie inside my head that told me I could change him with the money and total devotion to him. Maybe if I made enough to make him happy, I could make him proud and he would finally see the light and marry me. Wishful and sick thinking, I know. I held on so desperately to a fantasy, for a day that would never come.

The desperate desire I had for love and my low self-worth were the perfect ingredients for Julian's psychological manipulation, even in light of the violence. A relationship between a pimp and a prostitute has similar traits of Stockholm syndrome (named after a 1973 bank hostage situation in Sweden), where a victim emotionally bonds with her captor. When captives don't see a way out of their situation, they stay, developing an unhealthy and dependent attachment, being obedient in hopes of gaining love or security. In hostage situations, those held captive often begin to empathize and sympathize with their captors, and in many ways the same thing happens to sex-trafficking victims.

This is all very painful for me to talk about. It's not fun to share with you how naïve, stupid, and brainwashed I was. It's heartbreaking to actually have to write down that, yes, I really did sell myself to gain love. But I know I'm not the only one, and I know this is not the only way we sell ourselves. How many of us have sold ourselves in a different way without realizing it?

People date or even marry someone for money or favors or to fulfill an emotional need. Many of us compromise our worth, our integrity, our standards by exchanging it for a temporary fix to feel better. Whenever we trade or sell away the life God has in store for us, we "prostitute" ourselves.

I was a player in the game, an underground culture dominated by pimps who own their hoes. Within the pimp-prostitute framework, there is a system of ritual rules you have to abide by in order to live. You learn them as you go. Do the wrong thing and you get beaten. There's rarely or never a warning. So why didn't I run? Go to the police? Hightail it back to my parents? Run back to Kimmie's? Julian said I could leave whenever I wanted. After my first beatdown, that's exactly what I wanted to do—run. But Julian was always quick to remind me of the consequences if I left. He would hunt me down. And he would find me. The threats of physical harm as well as psychological and verbal threats are a powerful motivator. Knowing that you can lose your life or be maimed because you exercised your freedom isn't exactly inspiration to take off.

This is domestic violence with a horrific twist. You sell your body to guarantee that your boyfriend won't beat you or treat you like a slave, but ironically, you become the slave in the long run. You are a "good ho" when you do exactly what your pimp says; you are a "bad ho" when you don't. There is always a price to pay when you don't make enough money, when you talk back, when you think and act independently from what his plans are for you within the game.

I didn't even feel safe going to the police. First, I knew Julian was on the run, so I didn't want to get in trouble for harboring a criminal. Second, since we started dating, Julian made the cops out to be the enemy. Who would believe a prostitute? If anything, they'd probably throw me in jail.

Julian also created within me a dependence on him from the start. He took away my identification after that beating. Going forward, I wasn't allowed to open a credit card or bank account in my name. I couldn't even if I tried because I didn't have any proof of identification on me. And he would always tell me, "I'm the only one who loves and cares for you. No one is ever going to love you . . . You're a whore."

I was scared to death. And I figured out pretty quickly, within the first few days of being broken, that I didn't have a lot of options. I believed the police were out to get me. I believed my family and friends would never accept me. I believed I would be killed if I even tried to leave. The fear was so strong, I learned to survive in the situation. With great determination, I worked hard to pull in a ton of money so we could start a new life, the real fairy tale, somewhere. So for the next five years, I became Julian's ho, his sex slave, naively assuming that I was the only one.

CHAPTER 5

THE PIMP GAME

*"I really want to control the whole whore. I want to be
the boss of her life, even her thoughts. I got to con them
that Lincoln never freed the slaves."*
—Iceberg Slim, Pimp

A pimp is a master manipulator. In fact, I've heard it said many times that *pimp* stands for "power in manipulating people." At first he acts charming and loving, playing the role of a devoted and committed boyfriend. Ultimately, these winning tactics are used to control and manipulate his prostitute and hold her captive by making her think she will lose his love if she doesn't do what he asks. More times than not, a prostitute is psychologically tricked into thinking that the pimp loves her, will protect her, and will take care of her for the rest of her life. In reality, the pimp pulls the strings through verbal, mental, and severe physical abuse. A pimp is the master, his girl a slave.

The pimp lifestyle objectifies and exploits women and normalizes sexual abuse. This is the pimp subculture, making physical, mental, emotional, and sexual abuse part of "the rules of the game." In all reality, the subculture is very similar to ritual abuse that is practiced by cults. My pimp had other pimp families he was friends with and learned from, who knew the rules within the game. They would get together and have meetings where they would exchange ideas of how to keep their ladies in check.

When I worked as a prostitute for my pimp, I wasn't allowed to keep any of the earnings for myself. So if I was going on calls and was having a bad day emotionally, mentally, or physically, I just had to suck it up and change my attitude to make money. I am not going to lie—at first it was extremely difficult to know that when men touched me, had sex with me, or sexually and physically abused me, I would not receive any of the money I made, because I would have to hand it over to my pimp. I called it "paid rape" because I was forced to work no matter what day it was or how I was feeling. And every dollar I made went right into Julian's pocket. The more I had to do this for my pimp, the more I forced my angry feelings down into the pit of my stomach, and my tough girl personality, Fallen, took over.

In fact, eventually I became a dominance mistress with black leather clothes, fetish toys, and whips as my weapons. Honestly, I never intended to choose this specialized escort positional path, because it had started out only as an experiment. One night my escort service had an abundance of calls for men who were requesting dominance. They were short-handed so I decided to try it once—but then I realized that it was very easy playing the dominant, because I did not have to have sex with men, rather I would get paid to whip them. I think deep down inside it fed into the anger that had already been festering against the men who had abused me.

Like me, most of the prostitutes I knew had a pimp but were connected with an escort agency, which procured their clients. Today's mainstays of technology were pretty much nonexistent in the late eighties. People used phone books, not Google, to search for sexual entertainment. You could hire call girls by looking up "escort services" or "entertainment agencies" in the Yellow Pages or by dialing up the companies advertised in printed local magazines and newspapers. You could also find girls for hire by asking the concierges of the hotels, the VIP hosts, bartenders, and limo and taxicab drivers. In Las Vegas, many of the strip employees were on the take, making money off the ladies of the night in one form or the other—they all made their cut.

Escort/entertainment agencies, which marketed dancers or strippers for bachelor and other parties, were basically pretext for prostitution. They would never admit this truth, but all the girls working for the service knew what was going on.

In the pimp game, the girls rarely referred to themselves or each other as prostitutes. The terms we used most were *escort*, *ho*, or *sex worker*. There was also an understood hierarchy in place. The girls who walked the streets, or in pimp terminology "walked the track," were at the bottom of the pecking order. That's how I started out in Hawaii. There were also "carpet walkers" who strolled around the casinos, planting themselves near potential johns at the bars or playing tables in the casinos. This is what I did when I first visited Vegas with Kimmie and her boyfriend. There were also "freelancers," prostitutes who had a pimp but weren't associated with an escort agency and sought out their own clients.

Then there were the "renegades," working girls who didn't have a pimp and worked solo. This was a hated breed, and they were few and far between. If you didn't have a pimp, you were disrespecting the game. According to pimp rules, if a renegade so much as looked in a pimp's direction, he had the right to "charge" her, or to take her money and break her. Pimps typically preyed on green renegades unfamiliar with the rules of the game.

Most of my time with Julian consisted of working. My days were the same. I would wake up around 8:00 p.m., eat dinner, jump in the shower, and get ready for work, slipping into a sexy and trendy outfit that showed off my curves. I'd call my agency, and the operator would give me a list of dates for that night, starting with something like, "Hi, Fallen, I have a call for you lined up in room number 20-115 at the Mirage." Then I'd make my rounds up and down the hotels on the Strip. I checked in periodically with the agency during the night on my new cell phone Julian had given me a week after moving to Las Vegas, a Radio Shack Motorola. Having a cell phone, which at that time was rare for anyone other than the rich or elite to have, made me feel like I had arrived . . . important, special.

I'd go on an average of ten calls a night, including single tricks and bachelor parties where I'd have more than one client in a call. Similar to the strip clubs, all kinds of men called the escort service, every single Tom, Dick, and Harry you can imagine. I had young clients and old ones, businessmen, college students, married men, single men, celebrities. From janitors to judges, from politicians to movie stars, from blue-collar workers to the rich and famous—all these men paid to get something from us girls. I'd even get calls from fathers who wanted me to take their sons' virginity.

I worked nonstop every day. During the night I only took one break, using twenty minutes or so to scarf down some nearby fast food. If I was lucky, clients would order room service and I'd get to enjoy a juicy filet mignon or a gourmet Kobe burger. I was back home with Julian between six and eight in the morning after making my drop at the escort company.

The entire time I was with Julian I only had a handful of days off. I rarely took a vacation. I wasn't allowed any sick days (outside of needing to nurse myself to health and allow bruises and cuts to heal after violent beatings). I wasn't allowed to go home and visit my family. As lonely as I was and as much as I hated being apart from them, my relationship and the life I had didn't leave much room for family time—or much else. I worked hard to bring in money for my pimp, naively and foolishly hoping I would one day make enough to make him pull out of the game and marry me. Donna Summer's hit single "She Works Hard for the Money" was my theme song.

On average, I pulled in about $3,000 a night above the agency fees. I had some good nights where I raked in $10,000 or more and some crappy ones where I made as little as $1,500. In the five years I worked for Julian, I had one of the highest numbers of repeat clients in the agency. I was also the most requested because I looked so young and I was busty. I can't tell you how many calls came in requesting girls who were barely eighteen. Underage girls were particularly hot commodities.

As a call girl, I was a man's fantasy. I could be whatever he wanted me to be, with no strings. While many times I subconsciously felt guilty and ashamed about being the object of a man's lust that was so strong he was willing to cheat on his wife, Fallen would always push me aside and assure me that I needed to stop getting emotional and make money instead. Besides, it wasn't always just about the sex. I had many clients I got to know on an emotional level. They didn't just pay me for some action; they bought my companionship. This was one aspect of being an escort that made the experience more personal. I didn't just know what their fetishes were. I knew what they did for a living. I knew how many kids they had and what their names were. I knew their marriage struggles. I knew their stories. As twisted as this sounds, I felt justified being there as a sort of "sexual counselor."

I remember one middle-aged man who would always come to Vegas on the holidays. He called the escort services simply looking for companionship on Christmas Eve. A very lonely, shy, and broken man, this guy was desperate for female attention. He never wanted to have sex; he just needed someone to talk to and take out for dinner.

The money flowed hard and fast. Because I was desperate to please Julian and bring home stacks of cash, hoping it was enough to make him happy, I'd squeeze out as much money as I could from tricks. I was good. I knew how to talk. I knew how to turn on the charm. I knew how to determine how much I would charge. A large part of the game was getting the most money for doing the least amount of work. It was a vicious hustle.

My fee varied per client, depending on how rich he was. It was easy to spot a man with money. I could initially size up a man's wallet by giving him a once-over. Was he wearing a Rolex? Gucci loafers? I could make an even better assessment after a few steps into the room. Were there designer suits hanging in his closet? Bottles of expensive champagne on the dresser? Diamond cuff links on the nightstand? Sometimes the evidence of wealth was overt, with half-inch bank-strapped stacks of hundreds or nondescript paper bags stuffed sloppily with cash lying on the desk. The richer the john, the more I charged.

A few months after working for Julian, I went on a call at one of the suites in the opulent and spacious Caesar's Palace. A heavyset Jewish man in his fifties greeted me and welcomed me into the luxurious suite featuring a sprawling marble bar and sleek white-and-gold décor with about twenty bottles of Dom Pérignon and Cristal scattered around glass tabletops. *Cha-ching!* I quoted him $3,000 for the hour, to which he nodded and started counting out the bills one by one on an ornate gold side table. The man was sweating, perspiration sliding down the sides of his rotund face. I could tell he was high on cocaine, the drug of choice at the time.

He kindly walked me farther into the open-floored suite that boasted panoramic windows showcasing the sparkling Vegas skyline and a bubbling, steaming hot tub on the balcony.

The coke made it impossible for him to do anything sexual, so we sat in his bedroom watching the porno movie that was already on when I walked in. An hour passed, then two. I learned this man was an art dealer of Pablo Picasso's and Salvador Dali's works. He told me he had some friends staying with him in the suite and asked if I could send over other girls to party, which I did with a quick call to the agency. I stayed for a total of about four hours and walked out that night pocketing $12,000 and a few bottles of champagne as parting gifts.

The starless Las Vegas night was strangely cool when I left Caesar's Palace and headed home that night. I had the window down on my red convertible to pull a whiff of the fresh desert air. My ten-inch woofers in the back were booming to the beat of Janet Jackson as she sang, "Nasty boys, don't mean a thing." I had dead presidents stuffed in my bra, my take-home pay. I was completely exhausted and couldn't wait to get home, take a long, hot shower, and get the stench of the men off me. Yes, I had to hand over the money, but it was worth it because I couldn't wait to see my man.

As high as I was from the buzz of making good money that night at Caesars Palace, a few weeks later I would almost lose my life to a client turned psycho. I went on a call to the 22nd floor of the Sahara hotel at 2 a.m. in the morning. Because the man was inebriated and high on cocaine, he was unable to perform so he wanted his money back. Before I knew it, he threw me down on the bed, jumped on me, and started to choke me. I was in shock!

Instinctively, I took my right knee and kicked him where it counted, and after he fell to the floor, writhing in pain, I ran to grab my clothes and my purse. But as I was ready to run for the door, he got back up and grabbed both of my arms in a vise grip. And then the unthinkable happened—he picked me up, headed to the open window, and attempted to throw me out of it!

"Nooooooo! Heeeeeelp!" I screamed at the top of my lungs, and then I went into survival mode! I took my long nails to grab his eyes and started to gouge them with all my might. He dropped me instantly, and I raced toward the door. But he snatched my hair and yanked my back. As I was falling to the floor, I grabbed a lamp that was close by, and with all my might I smashed it against his head. *Crack!* He hit the ground with a huge thud, blood oozing from his forehead as he looked at me, dazed. I ran for the door again, and as he reached for my legs to

stop me, I kicked him in his face and yelled, "Ahhhhhhhhhh! Take that, you JERK!"

When I got in the hall, I screamed at the very top of my lungs, "Somebody help! Please—somebody, anybody!" I heard a door open just down the hall, and an elderly couple slowly peeked their heads out, shocked to see a naked women with a broken nose, bleeding face, black eye, and bruised neck. The elderly lady retrieved a robe to cover me and a towel to stop my bleeding, and I was taken into their room. As I explained through hysterical sobs what had just happened to me, they listened with such empathy and no judgment.

Security was called, and they arrived in less than two minutes. After a report was filled out, at least twenty minutes had gone by. I asked them if they would recover my things for me. We approached the room together and as a security officer knocked on the trick's door, he shouted, "SECURITY! OPEN UP!"

No answer. He repeated himself two more times. Then he proceeded to open the door. The man was gone, along with all of his luggage. The room had been tuned upside down and there was blood on the walls. I was really upset! Not just because he left without getting in trouble—but also because he had my things! *Everything* . . . including my money!

As I began to cry, the door opened up and another security guard slowly walked in and, with great sympathy in his eyes and voice, he said, "I've found your things—they are at the bottom of the Sahara." But no money. And my pager and phone were in a hundred pieces.

As I drove away from the hotel, I was completely broken and in total shock at what had just taken place. Then anger rose within me. I was so angry! Angry at the escort service, angry with the trick, and angry at myself. The escort service was supposed to watch over me and be my protector, but they'd left me hanging! The trick got away, and I couldn't call the police to press charges because I was at risk of getting arrested by vice.

And what would I tell Julian? How would he react? When I told him what had happened, I expected sympathy, comfort, and maybe enough rage to hunt that trick down and get my money back. Julian was angry all right, but not at the trick. All he did was tell me how disappointed he was in me and that I needed to learn how to be a smarter ho. This left me defeated and confused—I thought pimps were suppose to protect their women!

After that night, I determined to never let Julian know when a trick took advantage of me or threatened my life. Calls that turn violent are not uncommon in the sex industry; in fact, I know of thirteen women—some friends, some co-workers— who were killed in this lifestyle or just went missing.

———•———

Being with Julian as his bottom girl felt like being trapped in a web. It sucked the life out of me, draining me of my dreams and any hope. But Julian was like my vampire, keeping me alive in the midst of despair. I lived and breathed for his love, for that close-ness. Intimacy. When I left home for work at night, it was like leaving my coffin. I'd dress up and meet with men who would shower me with compliments and tell me how gorgeous I was. I admit that I ate up their words. But the minute tricks would touch me, no matter how much adoration or lust they poured out, my skin would start to crawl. I felt dirty, shameful, disgusting. I felt lost, like I was losing my mind, because my heart was often with my pimp.

When I got back home after a night of working, Julian resurrected me. He was my comfort, my saving grace. The feelings of repulsion disappeared. I felt okay again. My love for him, regardless of how toxic and twisted and sick, kept me going. I truly believe that unhealthy desire is one of the main reasons girls who are trafficked in the sex industry stay with their pimps so long, even when there are no bars on the doors or the windows; it's the chains on their hearts that keep them trapped.

The entire time I worked for Julian, I never drank or did drugs before, during, or after a trick while I was working on my shift. I didn't need to get high because my perverse love for Julian was my drug. I believed that the more I earned for our nest egg (nonexistent though I didn't know it at the time), the closer I'd be to getting a ring on my finger. This inspired and fueled me. My thought at the time was that doing dope was something only cheap hookers did. And as a high-class call girl, I wouldn't be caught dead snorting, shooting, or slamming back something that would make me look foolish or do stupid things. The only time I had a few drinks was when Julian and I hit the clubs to celebrate my earnings, something we did frequently early on.

There was a lot to celebrate. Namely, I was a cash cow. The first year I worked for Julian, he bragged on me to all of his pimp friends, so much that I quickly gained a reputation on the streets of Las Vegas as a moneymaker. I made Julian an average of $20,000 a week, every week. That's $84,000 a month, $1,092,000 a year (or over $2 million today!). That's a lot of money made fast!

So where did the money go? Julian didn't give me a dime, though he bought me clothes and cars and gave me a place to live. But I couldn't keep what he bought if I decided to leave one day for good. Oh, and he'd give me a twenty every night before I left home so I could stock up on condoms and use the remaining few bucks at McDonald's or another cheap fast food place.

Truth was, I didn't know where all the money went. The first time I asked Julian, he punched me and told me to shut my trap. I learned that day that asking your pimp about his handling of finances was disrespectful and demanded a beatdown. I did know he liked to gamble and play high-roller games at the Mirage and Caesars, to name a couple. He also liked having nice things, like his tailored Armani and Gucci suits, diamond chains, designer this, designer that, and didn't mind indulging me in high fashion and pricey jewelry, especially because it propped up my image of being a top-dollar escort.

So yeah, all that work and nothing to show for it. This reminds me of a verse in the Bible that says, "Wealth gained hastily will dwindle, but whoever gathers little by little will increase it" (Proverbs 13:11 ESV).

On the flip side, bringing in that kind of money bolstered my confidence, even though I pocketed none of it. Ironic, isn't it? It filled the void of my absent self-esteem. And it was something I did very well. I remember making a drop at the Shark Club, a hot dance venue on the corner of Harmon Avenue and the Strip (back then, the clubs were outside of the casinos and hotels). The music blared in my ears as I marched into the joint with my sky-high heels, a little black dress, and a pair of glimmering chandelier earrings. Julian sat on a blood-red leather couch with his buddies, all of them decked out in Italian custom suits, nodding their heads and tapping their alligator-skin shoes to the beat.

Julian saw me walk his way and started nudging his pimp friends, saying, "My top girl in Vegas is back," and smiling approvingly. "I know she clocked me some money!" Then he made a big scene out of counting the stack of bills I had made that night, showing off the trap in front of his friends. He smiled and hugged and kissed me passionately, proud. There was something about his smile, the look of joy on his face from seeing the money that made me feel like a good girl. It motivated me to keep up the good work. Money changed Julian. It made him happier, less on edge, definitely less violent. I was determined to use that currency to keep him happy.

There were a handful of times we'd celebrate the cash and dance for hours at the hottest nightclubs like Tramps, the Palladium, and Sharks. I felt like a queen those nights, arm in arm with my man, owning the dance floor with our slick moves while covered in bling, sparkling diamonds, and gold chains. Back then, we didn't have VIP rooms as private and highly guarded as we have now. All the celebrities, rock stars, and other "important" people hung out in roped-off dark corners. Sometimes we planted ourselves in that elite crowd; other times we stationed ourselves with the other pimps and their girls, decked out in the best clothes and popping bubbly. Those moments were few, and the fun I believed I experienced was deceiving. Instinctively, I knew a fleeting few hours of dancing and champagne couldn't mask the truth, that I was someone's sex-trafficked slave.

Having sex for money came with its risks, and one was being thrown behind bars. I was arrested the first time in 1989. The agency sent my girlfriend Rosey and me on a call together at the Stardust. My hair was bleached at the time and flowed down my back thanks to hair extensions. Two handsome men in their early thirties wearing sports coats and slacks greeted us warmly and invited us into their room. After they handed us the agency fee ($150) and $500, we took off our clothes. But instead of them doing the same, they pulled out their police badges. *Vice cops!* "Put your clothes on," came the command, as well as the reading of our Miranda rights. The cops joked and laughed with each other, not making a big deal of the arrest. I, however, did not share their lighthearted attitude. Tears welled up in my eyes. I was embarrassed. Ashamed. I felt dirty, ugly. As one of the cops slapped the cold, steel handcuffs around my wrists and charged me with solicitation, I was practically shaking in my white, patent leather, spiked high heels. I wasn't mad at them for doing their job. I was afraid of them. My fear stemmed from Julian's words that rang in my ears. Cops were the bad guys, out to get me. I was on the wrong side of the law.

Walking out of the Stardust flanked by two cops was mortifying. I put my head down, ignoring what I knew were stares bearing down on me. The fifteen-minute ride to the Clark County Detention Center was an annoying question-and-answer session. The detectives drilled us with questions: Why were we selling our bodies? . . . Did we have boyfriends and, if so, did they know what we were doing? . . . Were we paying our boyfriends' bills or giving them money?

I lied. I told them I held all the money and that I was saving for college so I could study music. Behind the glass partition, they both laughed and said that the man I was with was most likely feeding me pipe dreams, that he was going to take advantage of me and probably beat the living daylights out of me as soon as I didn't comply with his wishes. They were right, but I didn't let them know it. I shrugged my shoulders. I knew they wanted me to give up my pimp's name. But I was no snitch.

I was thrown in a twenty-by-twenty cement holding tank, filled shoulder to shoulder with fellow prostitutes, drunk drivers, crackheads, and drug dealers. Long benches lined two walls on opposite sides with every inch of wooden space taken by hard-looking working girls sporting wild eighties hair and long red fingernails. A dirty metal toilet and sink occupied a corner, separated from the rest of the cell by thin dividers, one of which had a tiny opening where outsiders could peer in and see the person, from the chest up, relieving themselves on the toilet. It was humiliating. We were all given numbers and had to wait for our turn to be booked, fingerprinted, and questioned. Some of the girls tried to persuade me to come and work for their pimp. "You wanna come home to my daddy?" one asked. "He'll treat you real good and spoil you with nice things. Come on, girl, you need to get with a real man and family, one that's gonna help you come up." I ignored the bait. I wasn't interested. There was only one man for me—Julian.

When a loudmouthed officer shouted my name, I shoved my way through the clamoring crowd of noisy women to be further hammered by questions about who I worked for.

"You got a pimp, Lobert?"

I shook my head. "No, sir."

"You lying to us, Lobert?"

"No, sir, I have a boyfriend."

I used my one phone call to call Julian. "I went on a bust tonight. You need to make my bail and get me out." I was released almost twenty-four hours later. Julian paid the $200 bail and drove me home so I could get some sleep. In my time as a prostitute, I was arrested a total of twenty-five times, the majority of those incidences while I was with Julian. The prostitution vice cops were on to me. They knew I had a hellacious guerilla pimp who was very violent so they would harass me to see if I would snitch or fold on him. But in the game, you don't snitch or you are as good as dead. Just like the Italian mafia.

———— • ————

The life in the subculture of pimping is also a polygamist society. Pimps build stables, their families of girls. The one they usually live with—who has been with them the longest and is considered the most loyal—is called the "bottom girl," which is what I was to Julian. She is in charge when the pimp is away. The other girls are known as the "wife-in-laws" or "wifey." Every girl in the stable must adore her pimp and completely surrender to him. She must worship him, follow the pimp's rules, do whatever he says, and, of course, turn over all the money she makes.

A year and a half or two years after moving to Vegas with Julian, the first girl in our stable, at least to my knowledge, showed up with him fresh off the plane from Minneapolis. The night I broke my trap, when I surrendered all my money to him, I suspected there were other girls but didn't want to believe it. I shoved away those suspicions, choosing to believe instead the false dream of true love. And even if there were other women, I was determined to be the only one he would be in love with.

This girl was eighteen. A beautiful, tall, and lanky brunette. She was shy and most of the time kept her eyes toward the ground. I was instantly jealous of her, my biggest fear being that this chick would replace me as Julian's bottom girl, but I had no say in the matter.

A Louis Vuitton garment bag in one hand, his other clasping the girl's beautifully manicured hand, Julian barked his orders to me: "You're going to turn her out!" (In other words, train her—sign her up at the escort agency, teach her the rules of the game, show her how it's done.) I nodded, keeping my protests and anger silent. I knew if I got upset or showed even the slightest hint of jealousy, he'd likely bash in my face. I wasn't in the mood to get sassy and take a chance.

The girl stayed with us for a few weeks. Surprisingly, the more I got to know this girl, the more I liked her. She was a sweetheart. It was hard for me to hate her, no matter how pissed off I was that I wasn't Julian's only girl. She was so young, so sweet, so fresh. It pained me to know she was part of the game. "Why are you here?" I asked her in our first few days together. "You shouldn't be, darling. Go back home. Trust me, you don't belong here." She refused, telling me she loved Julian. I could only imagine the lines he fed her, probably the same ones he fed me. When a pimp is trying to win a girl, he plays a hard romance. I didn't want to believe it was true, but I saw the love in her eyes for Julian, the same glint I had in mine in the beginning. It made me sick to my stomach.

I couldn't keep quiet too long. A week after she showed up, I complained to Julian. I couldn't contain my jealousy and questioned his intentions and his commitment to me. Julian, of course, denied any affection for her, claiming she was just his working girl and I was his beloved bottom girl. "I only love you, Fallen, you know that. Remember our dreams, baby, that's what I'm trying to do here. Back me up, don't be against me."

When the evidence of Julian pimping other girls was thrown in my face, a part of me was terrified about getting caught by the police. Because I was a part of Julian's stable, I could have been charged with pimping and pandering (today it's called sex trafficking) unless I agreed to "snitch" Julian out to the vice cops. So I kept quiet, kept my mouth shut. Other girls showed up over time. Some stayed for a few months; others cycled out quicker. None of the girls lived with us, however, so I continued to claim my status as Julian's one and only.

The truth is, I felt sorry for the other girls. I befriended them. I didn't want them to get hurt. I knew what Julian was capable of, and to think he could do to others what he had done to me was ever so frightening. I even helped ship a few girls away, particularly the ones who were underage, encouraging them to return home. Many of them were scared, though they tried to act hard and tough. I could see they wanted out so I helped them and covered for them. On several occasions I lied straight to Julian's face and pretended I was outraged when we discovered a girl or two missing over the years. He never found out the truth, that I was the one motivating them to leave and helping with their escapes.

It was more than just other prostitutes Julian was after when we were together. He had a deep-seated porn addiction. I caught him many times watching it when I came home from work. It disgusted me, made me sick to my stomach.

I was so jealous of the girls on the screen. I didn't want Julian to desire anyone but me. I couldn't compete with the fantasies he watched, or the fantasies he acted out in real life. One day Julian handed me a thick photo album. "Here are some punk girls I've known," he said, proudly displaying the open book on the coffee table. I opened it up and flipped through page after page of Polaroid shots of his sexual conquests, some women naked, others partly clothed, all in provocative poses. There were hundreds of photos of women of every color, size, and age. I was in the book as well, a picture I had never intended to be exploited in this way.

It's hard to love a pimp. Even though I was the bottom girl, I always believed there was someone else who was going to replace me, a new girl somewhere who would vie for and win his attention and affection. He played the same song-and-dance routine time after time, telling me I was the only one, but the cajolery was getting old. By the time a few years had passed since we met, I was getting tired of the game, for more reasons than just the other women.

One night I walked in the door of our brand-new second-floor condo, complete with an elegant fireplace, Italian black leather couches, and a spacious terrace overlooking the sparkling pool below. I set down a mouthwatering, finger-licking-good rack of BBQ-slathered ribs on the kitchen counter top. Julian was sitting on the couch, watching our big-screen TV. I pulled out my trap and handed it to him with a big smile on my face. I knew he'd be pleased with the thick wad of cash. He counted the money slowly, methodically, and set it down. Then he walked toward me, smiling. But the smile wasn't a happy one. It was the sick kind.

Julian looked at me with the familiar calm-before-the-storm stare and said, "Loose lips sink ships, ho!" I knew what was coming next, though I didn't know why. Right after those words spewed from his mouth, he pushed me down on the white carpet and started choking me, and I knew his rage wouldn't subside until there were broken bones, bruises, and blood. I blacked out, and when I groggily drifted back into consciousness, I heard him say, "You talking about my business?!" I tried to get up, but was knocked down by his steel-toed boot.

The screaming ensued. "Keep your mouth shut about our business in the streets!" He stood on top of me, bearing all of his weight down on my chest. I heard a rib crack as I struggled to breathe. It felt like a thousand knives were stabbing me, and my heart was about to burst. Julian was "stomping me" for punishment, for breaking a rule. But this all happened because of a lie. Another pimp, who knew that Julian had a hot temper, wanted him to beat me and thus keep me out of work for a week or two. It was a strategy that the pimps sometimes played on each other to mess each other's money up. I can't say how long this beating lasted because it all became a blur as I was battered in and out of consciousness.

A few hours later I woke up in my bed, alone. Julian had taken off on a trip, to Minnesota I think, and had asked his nineteen-year-old nephew, Bobby, to take care of me. I hurt so bad I was pretty sure I had internal bleeding. I definitely knew my ribs were cracked (to this day my top rib sticks out). But I couldn't go to the hospital for fear of someone finding out who had beaten me. Bobby was a loving, gentle-hearted soul. For the next two to three weeks, he was my doctor, nurse, and caretaker, hovering over me with kindness while I moaned, bedridden. He fed me. He made me drink water. He even carried me to the bathroom a few times a day. And he voiced his concern.

"Fallen," Bobby would tell me multiple times as he sat beside me on the edge of the bed. "You're going to die if you stay here. Unc is going to end up really hurting you, or killing you."

I knew he was right. I knew the beatings, the abusive relationship, and my sick love for the violent man who sold me for sex were wrong. I cannot adequately describe to you the emotional turmoil I experienced. If you've never been in an abusive love relationship, the perverse dynamic is difficult to understand. I was not only imprisoned out of fear that Julian would hunt me down and kill me if I left him, I was also emotionally attached and in love with the guy. I still didn't want to believe that he was a monster. My relationship with him was a lot like the relationship between Christine and the Phantom of *Phantom of the Opera*. Instead of singing, I wanted to believe he would change if I just could be a better prostitute for him. I was already doing the best I could by working every single night and bringing home thousands of dollars. But clearly it wasn't enough.

Julian came back a few weeks later, showering me with roses and diamonds. "I love you, baby," he whispered in my ear, holding me close to him as I winced in pain from the embrace. "We can make this work, honey. We're going to have a better life one day. I promise." He even apologized for the beating, telling me he had foolishly chosen to believe a false rumor spoken by that jealous pimp friend of his.

Sadly, this beating wasn't the turning point. But something in me finally started to disbelieve the lies, the false promises, the meaningless words of apology and vows to change. I began to wake up at that point, accepting a glimmer of the dark truth. And oh, how dark it was! I began to question my sanity and my safety, and knew that the time was drawing near when I would have to start planning my escape—that I would have to start stashing money and possibly change my identity to get away from the monster I had fallen in love with.

Girls can't just leave their pimps, and many of my friends are no longer alive to tell their stories of attempted escapes. One girl I knew who was being violently abused by her pimp was found dead a few states away, a bullet shot through her head. Though he was never charged or arrested, we all knew her pimp killed her. It was practically common knowledge on the street.

The entire time I was with Julian, he both wooed and threatened me with his words and actions. He had an impressive collection of guns. Every now and then, when I would get out of line or sass him with my big mouth, he'd load up a gun, wave it around, and tell me stories of people he had harmed, usually former associates whom he needed to keep under his thumb. I believed him. Why wouldn't I? I saw how he hurt me. I knew his temper and his intense rage.

Julian made sure I was isolated. He kept me away from my family and friends, anyone who wasn't a part of the game. He didn't want me interacting with anyone who could possibly talk some sense into me. While I lived in Las Vegas, I saw my family back home on only a handful of occasions. No one ever found out about my lifestyle, though Julian would laugh and make snide comments like, "What would happen if your daddy found out what you do for a living? He'd probably have a nervous breakdown!"

It was during these times—the threats, the beatings, the criticizing—that I wish I could have left. I just didn't have enough strength, posture, guts, sense, whatever you want to call it, to run from the battlefield. I couldn't figure out how to escape the web of abuse, but knew I needed to. I began to think, to plan, to figure out how I could slip away seamlessly, like in a spy movie, and make a new life somewhere else. I knew it would take time, but if I didn't do it, I was afraid the next beating would be my last.

CHAPTER 6

RUNAWAY GIRL

"My dear sister, you can't escape God, and you can't escape your skeletons in the closet. They will always be there until you take them out."
—Corallie Buchanan

About a year and a half before I left Julian, I started stashing money away, a hundred bucks at a time. I hid some bills under a small, ripped-up piece of carpet underneath an oversized marble Corinthian pedestal that held a stone statute. I stashed some under the carpet in my car. One of the phone girls at the escort agency, whom I had befriended over the years, got tired of witnessing the cycle of abuse and seeing my face caked with heavy Dermablend concealer to cover up the bruises and welts. She wanted to help and safeguarded some cash for me.

Things between Julian and me were getting worse. The beatings were getting more frequent, and we weren't going out to celebrate anymore. Life was a blur of tricks and anxiety-ridden moments outside of work. I feared Julian's next move and could sleep only with the help of Tylenol PM, my faithful bedtime companion.

So when Julian asked me to drive up to Minneapolis to meet him, a frequent travel spot where he would sometimes stay as long as a month or two, I chomped at the bit. Okay, so it wasn't a vacation, and the only reason I was going was to drop off some money for him ($20,000, to be exact), but it was time away from the lights, from the johns, from the fog of thousands of hotel rooms that had all started to look the same. It was time on long stretches of highways to breathe. And think.

A tall brunette named Jean came along so she could meet up with her pimp, a friend of Julian's who also had some roots in Minneapolis. I drove the new white Mustang convertible Julian had bought me (with my money, of course) for thirteen hours straight, staying awake courtesy of Boyz II Men, C+C Music Factory, and Color Me Badd on maximum volume. But thirteen hours is a long time. And I was fading fast.

Jean, who had just gotten her driver's license, noticed my head slowly nodding off and piped up from the white leather passenger seat, "Girl, switch with me. You look tired." Though I wasn't thrilled to let a newbie driver take the wheel of my brand-new car, I wasn't going to argue with her. My eyelids felt so heavy, like barbells bearing down on my face.

We pulled over on a Colorado highway, taking a few minutes to stretch our arms and bask in the clear blue sky as midmorning traffic whizzed by. Then we hit the road. Jean rocked out the Mustang with more R&B and dance tunes. I reclined the passenger seat and put my feet up on the dashboard, closing my eyes and hoping to catch up on some beauty sleep so I could look fresh for my man.

I woke abruptly from a five-minute catnap to the sound of Jean swearing loudly and exclaiming, "I dropped my lighter" as she reached down with one hand trying to locate it. By the time I sat up to search for the lighter among the pile of scattered CDs, she had already put her head down to look for the lighter. With Jean's eyes off the road, the car veered into the oncoming lane. Feeling the violent shift in direction, I gasped and looked up just in time to hear the blaring horn of a semitrailer truck heading toward us. I screamed, and Jean jerked the car back into its original lane. At eighty miles an hour, the Mustang started circling out of control, furiously spinning out in donuts in the middle of the freeway. My stomach reeled from the nonstop revolutions. As the car started slowing down its circles, it rolled over, landing upside down on its hood with a crashing thud on top of a three-foot-wide rock. That rock saved our lives. Only the front half of the car rested on it, so there was space between the ground and the car, enough room so our heads hadn't been crushed.

Jean and I managed to walk out of the crash with just minor cuts and bruises. Shaken from what could have been a deadly accident, we numbly sat on the side of the road waiting for help, staring at the mangled mess of metal and shards of glass littering the highway's shoulder. We didn't say much, just stared at the totaled car. We were in shock, I think. Ten minutes later a state trooper drove by. After exchanging information, he informed me that the insurance on the vehicle had run out the day before. Apparently Julian had forgotten to pay it.

I used the cash I had on hand to have the totaled Mustang towed back to Las Vegas. Jean and I hitched a ride with some dudes who drove us to nearby Denver where I used more money for a plane ticket to Minneapolis. Julian picked me up at the airport (Jean had already been picked up by her pimp), and we drove back to a downtown hotel to chill. He didn't seem too upset over the accident, just concerned that I was okay. We went to a club later that night, and Julian had a couple of drinks. With each rum and Coke he threw back, he seemed to get less lovey-dovey and more agitated. By the time it was last call, Julian wasn't Julian anymore.

As soon as we arrived in our hotel room and I heard the click of the door closing behind me, Julian let loose. He started beating the living daylights out of me. "You irresponsible—" he roared as he pounded his fists into my face. He started blaming me for the accident, for the lapse in car insurance, for having to shell out cash for the plane ticket to Minneapolis. With every word that came out of his mouth, his rage increased. As he choked me without restraint, blood flowed out of my mouth and my nose. I couldn't see Julian anymore. A tangible presence of hatred and disgust filled his eyes. I didn't recognize the man on top of me beating me. He looked like pure evil, as though he were possessed by a demon.

I blacked out and woke up in his car. Julian dropped me off at his sister's house, where I spent a few weeks recovering. I lay in bed, nursing more wounds (severe double protruding black eyes) and being tended to by this kind, sweet woman. She and I didn't talk much. I was a wreck, paralyzed by pain, by fear, by regret. I blamed myself for the beating. It's my fault the insurance lapsed. It's my fault I made him so angry. It's my fault I wasted his precious money. I knew my family wasn't far away, but there was no way I could see them looking like this. I'd only freak them out with the bruises and cuts on my face, neck and, well, everywhere. My parents had reached out over the years, begging me to fly out, but the timing was always off.

I was either too busy making money for Julian or too beaten up to see them.

I flew back to Las Vegas at some point. Julian came back on a separate flight, repeating the pattern of long-winded apologies. He cried. He admitted he was wrong. He bought me nice things. He begged me to forgive him, which I did, though reluctantly.

A few months later I decided enough was enough. More girls had come into the picture, though none lived with us. Julian started traveling even more (to pick up girls for his stable, I learned later). The lifestyle was too hard, too lonely, too heart-breaking. I couldn't take it anymore. I was done. It was time to leave.

I had saved up about seven grand at that point and had enlisted the help of a girlfriend who offered to let me stay with her until I could get back on my feet. I knew leaving was the right thing to do, but I was very nervous and afraid. At night I tossed and turned, wondering what my consequences would be. Would Julian find me? Kill me? Or could I disappear without a trace? I waited until my pimp was off on another trip to make my move.

The day he left, driven to the airport by one of his pimp friends, I watched his light-blue Mercedes-Benz pull out of the driveway and down the street. Once the image of the luxury car was a speck on the horizon, I got into gear, moving fast, my heart pounding.

I grabbed my luggage from the garage and ran upstairs to the master bedroom I shared with Julian. In a frenzy, I packed a bunch of my clothes and stuffed my purse with stacks of cash from my secret hiding places around the house. I also grabbed a diamond-faced watch Julian had custom-made for me as well as some diamond rings, shoving them hurriedly in my purse. I shut the door of the apartment behind me, not looking back, and took off for my friend's one-bedroom apartment. Though she lived right around the block, she had became my friend and was the only person I trusted at the time. She was a phone girl at the main escort service I worked for, and she always commented that if I ever wanted to leave my pimp, she would help me. I stayed with her for a month before I got my own place. Of course I was nervous he would spot me, but it was worth risking my life to try to find happiness again.

Julian left messages for me multiple times a day. He was like Dr. Jekyll and Mr. Hyde. Sometimes he would be sweet, promising things would get better and he would change. Then after a few voice mails like that, without a response from me, he'd start flipping out. The messages would turn into threatening ones. He'd say things like, "When I find you, I'm going to kill you. You think you're pretty slick, don't you? You think you can hide from me?" After a few days' worth of aggressive messages, he'd turn the charm back on, telling me I was his only woman and hint that we would be together forever. You get the drift. I didn't call him back. I was scared, avoiding the places he frequented. I kept a low profile and focused on creating my own life on my own terms.

I put most of the money I had saved on a lease option to buy a beautiful town home by a lake. I immediately fell in love with the vaulted ceilings, floor-to-ceiling windows, and the white marble floor that reflected elegance and wealth. Not to mention the huge master bedroom suite with a Jacuzzi tub and the adjoining balcony wrapped around with thick white banisters in the curvy shape of an hourglass. The townhouse was mine, all mine. I felt proud, accomplished, and hopeful, for the first time in a very long time.

The high wore off pretty quickly when reality set in. I had nothing to show for the roughly four and a half years I'd been working for Julian other than a beautiful, and relatively empty, place to live. I had to get back to work. But it wasn't so easy. I had lost more than money during that time. I lost my motivation to work because I finally saw my relationship for what it was—broken, sick, violent, and toxic. I lost my self-esteem and struggled with depression, content to just lie in bed all day in my huge bedroom instead of dragging out my sexy wear and fulfilling fantasies for thousands of dollars. I was also very tired. Every pore in my body, mind, and heart was sopped in exhaustion. The beatings, the johns, the emotional gymnastics, the lifestyle, the violence—all these things take an extreme toll on you.

I stopped working nights and tackled the day shift, which had a completely different level of energy, clientele, and money. For starters, it was safer because I could hide and lie low from Julian. He and his pimp friends, who would likely rat me out, were rarely out during the day. Unlike the night shift, most of the clientele were sober, or at least not so outrageously high or drunk that they couldn't perform the services they were paying for (though I did have the occasional johns who had been up all night snorting cocaine and weren't done partying just yet). Probably the biggest letdown was that the dayshift was slower, which meant less money, about a third to a half less than what I was bringing in before. Though I wasn't thrilled to be making less money, I took what I could get. I didn't have a choice. I needed the cash.

In addition to using my money for a place to live, I also bought a pearl-white Nissan Altima. I purposely chose a non-descript vehicle, something a square would likely drive, so I could be incognito. If Julian was looking for me on the Strip, he wouldn't be so quick to notice me in a non-flashy vehicle.

After a few months, I started resurfacing at night. I lay low and continued to work only a few nights a week. Though my zeal for selling myself had died down to a slower simmer, I was happy to be a high-class independent escort without a pimp. I had become one of those "renegades" in the game, doing things my way. I was going to somehow reach the point where I could save a couple hundred grand and transition my way out. To do what and go where, I hadn't a clue. Though I was proud of myself for gaining my independence, the truth was, I still hoped I'd find a rich john to take care of me, someone who would notice my true worth and beauty, sweep me off my feet, and take me away on a wild, white horse. Yeah, the Disney fantasy was still echoing in my heart, even though my life thus far had been the furthest thing from a fairy tale.

Not too long after being on my own, I found myself in another deadly situation, except this time it had nothing to do with my ex-boyfriend/pimp. One night I got a call from the phone girl at the agency. She was excited to tell me about a call for me at the Imperial Palace penthouse suite (today the hotel is called The Link). Dollar signs flashed before my eyes. As usual, I dressed to impress, donning a black, form-fitting Japanese Tadashi jumpsuit studded with Austrian crystals.

I knocked on the door, which was answered by a short Mexican man sporting an unflattering bowl haircut (think Jim Carrey's character in *Dumb and Dumber*). As I asked the man for ID, something I did regularly, I was overcome with a weird feeling in my gut. Something about this guy was off. He seemed on edge. His eyes darted around nervously without making eye contact with me. Most of the johns I met were friendly and inviting. After all, they were paying me for a service with a happy ending. If they wanted a good time, they had to play nice.

"Wait a minute," he answered in a thick accent. A minute later the man came back, but not with a driver's license. He pointed a .357 snub-nosed magnum revolver in my face. I stood paralyzed, staring at the short barrel only an inch away from my nose. One thought and one thought only crossed my mind: *Oh my God, I'm going to die as a call girl.*

"This is my ID!" the man snarled and motioned me inside the suite. In a forceful yet calm demeanor, he demanded that I take off my clothes and give him my purse. The gun still pointed at me, he awkwardly rummaged through my leather Gucci clutch with his free hand and stuffed $500 of my money into his jean's pocket. I stood before him in fear, naked, my beautiful outfit gathered into a wrinkly mess at my bare feet. He picked up my clothes, undergarments and all, and tossed them out the window.

Then the man shoved me into the bedroom and pushed me facedown on the bed, the metal weapon digging forcefully into my spine. I pleaded with him, "Why are you doing this? I'll do whatever you want. Just tell me!" Tears streamed down my face. I heard the familiar sound of a condom package unwrapping and then the force of his body into mine. My face was pressed into an embroidered silk decorative pillow, the beads pressing painfully into my cheeks, as he raped me. When it was all over, gun in hand, he told me to go into the bathroom and lay on the floor.

I had been raped many times before, but never with a gun. Rape without a weapon is petrifying. Adding a gun to the mix brings on a whole new level of fear. I didn't know what was going to happen as I lay naked on the bathroom floor, my only view being the curved bottom of a toilet. I was afraid for my life. For all I knew, my rapist planned to splatter my brains all over the sparkling marble tile. I don't know how much time passed before I got up. The penthouse was so spacious, I wouldn't have been able to hear if the guy left or was still in the suite. I took my chances.

Quietly standing up, I wrapped myself with a plush towel that hung on a golden hook on the bathroom door. I tiptoed around the place, looking for signs the man was still around. Luscious green plants adorned the suite in every corner, and colorful bouquets of tropical flowers decorated glass tabletops—beauty in the midst of violence.

I didn't hear a sound. I didn't see anyone. I continued to tiptoe my way around, looking past the elegantly set dining room table. My racing heart slowed to a manageable pace as I picked up the telephone, hand shaking, to report the rape to security. Before I had a chance to press "0," I heard the door to the penthouse open. I panicked. A well-dressed couple in their late sixties stood in the hall. The woman stared at me, her jaw dropping to the floor, while the man barked, "What are you doing here?"

I stood up, wrapped the towel tighter around my chest, and cried, "I just got raped in this room!"

The couple stood firm in the hallway, clearly not believing a word I said, and the man retorted, "This is our suite. I'm calling security."

I froze. How was I going to explain what just happened? On one hand, I had been raped, but on the other hand, I was on an escort call. When security arrived, pandemonium broke out. The couple, who had actually booked the suite, was raving mad, ranting about how some strange, naked woman had broken into their penthouse. I had to 'fess up and tell the security officer that I was a call girl. The minute I uttered the words, I felt humiliated.

"I have to call the police," he told me matter-of-factly. I begged the guy, "Please don't. Please!" The security officer ignored my pleas and told me to sit down on the couch and said that he'd be back. I was still in tears, shaking and sobbing, when he returned fifteen minutes later with my clothes and a vice cop. I begged the cop to let me go and surprisingly, he did. I immediately drove home and climbed into bed, pulling the covers over my head like a scared little girl afraid of the monsters in her closet. I was so traumatized by the whole experience that I called the escort agency and let them know I was done for the night. I couldn't work. I wasn't in the right headspace.

I carried that fear with me for a long time afterward, showing up to work wondering if that guy was ever going to reappear. I didn't just have Julian and the pimp mafia to watch out for anymore; now I also had to watch my back for my rapist.

I won't lie. I missed Julian. Life was lonely. And life, though relatively peaceful, was lacking in romance. I couldn't get high on love anymore. My drug, my man, was gone. I started missing the good times we had, the closeness I felt with Julian when he shared his life struggles and pain about his childhood, the times we talked about finally making it big and getting out of the life. Soon he stopped leaving hateful messages for me and went back into "Romeo" mode with countless messages telling me he missed and loved me and only wanted to be with me.

Well, unfortunately, his words dragged me back in. One day I finally called him. He gushed out dramatic apologies and begged me to take him back. He was sorry. I forgave. And then I did what I thought was an obvious next step—I suggested he move in with me in my beautiful new place. Honestly, I was hoping this would be a different relationship this time . . . as crazy as that sounds.

There's no denying it was a sick love and that my pull toward him was toxic. It's heartbreaking to remember how desperate I was to love the person I thought Julian could be one day and not who he really was. My passion for him was based on false ideals that were destined to crumble. But I wasn't ready to give up on him. I wasn't ready to give up on the fantasy of what could be. I held on for dear life to the hope of salvaging something potentially beautiful, whatever the cost.

We quickly dove into boyfriend-girlfriend mode, decorating the townhouse together with Egyptian art and even picking out an ornate chandelier we hung together in the foyer. I didn't ask what, if any, other girls were working for him. I'm sure they were around somewhere; I just never saw them. I didn't want to know. I needed to keep this magic bubble of our relationship intact. Out of sight, out of mind.

It didn't take long, however, for me to get the itch to leave. After a few days, I realized that he hadn't changed and that he was planning another trip to Minnesota to pick up some more work (girls/women). I questioned him about it, asking him why he had to go when we had just gotten back together and telling him that I didn't want this in our relationship anymore. You see, this is what typically happens when a woman falls in love with her pimp—she tries to change him into a square, in hopes that one day he won't be pimping any longer and decide to settle down with his bottom girl. My heart remembered the pain from before, and the thought of going through that heartache again was more than I could bear. I couldn't continue the relationship. The promises he vowed were empty, meaningless. I saw the light and woke up. You cannot pretend the truth doesn't exist when you see it for yourself.

Julian had no plans to start over with me. He certainly didn't change. He had plans to spend more time than before away from me, on secretive trips to God knows where. A leopard will never change his spots.

I didn't have an official escape plan this time; I was simply trying to figure out my options and the logistics in my head. Where would I stay? Who could I call this time? What would I do without a safety net of cash?

Somehow Julian got wind of my mental schemes. I don't know how. I hadn't told a soul about wanting to run away. I think he just knew me so well he could sense something was amiss. One day I was flipping through a magazine on the couch when he told me, "Come here! I got to go out of town. But I gotta do something first." He drew a gun out of the back of his jeans and, pointing it directly in my face, forced me into the garage.

Julian popped the trunk of the Benz and reached for a large piece of rope, which he started slowly and methodically wrapping around my hands. I cried. I pleaded, "Julian, what are you doing? This is crazy! Stop it!" Physically, he had me. I couldn't get away. As he told me to get in the trunk, my eyes fell on a heavy-duty black body bag and a metal shovel that glimmered in the dim light. I tried to scream, but Julian immediately clamped his hand over my mouth. I was horrified, letting out only muffled yelps. *Oh my God*, I thought, *he is finally going to make good on his promise to bury me in the desert.*

With the barrel of his gun digging into my back, I climbed into the trunk. Julian slammed it shut and started the car. I didn't hear the garage door open and panicked. *I am going to die of carbon monoxide poisoning.* As I lay on the heavy body bag, desperately trying to get the rope off my hands, I heard Julian start talking again. "Yeah, this is what you get for trying to plan. You think you're so slick, but I got you figured out! You think you can play me for a punk? You got another think comin'!" My heart raced. There wasn't anything I could do. I was trapped! About to die.

Then, in an inexplicable strange moment of calm, I thought of fond memories, peaceful ones. I thought of the mornings I'd eat candy and other treats while listening to Bible stories in Sunday school. I thought of the teacher telling me about Jesus, about how He was my friend. I thought of the songs I was taught about this Man. And with tears streaming down my face, in the middle of the darkness, I started singing at the top of my lungs.

Jesus loves me, this I know
For the Bible tells me so

Little ones to Him belong
They are weak but He is strong
Yes, Jesus loves me
Yes, Jesus loves me
Yes, Jesus loves me
The Bible tells me so

Dumbfounded by my antics, Julian roared, "What the—?" He turned off the car immediately after I belted out the last word in the song and got me out of the trunk. He looked at me, shook his head, and said, "You really are crazy. Get back in the house, girl." Then he packed up his stuff and left on one of his trips. That night I left Julian and my new home I had worked so hard to get. I stayed with another friend for a few weeks to regain my independence. Again.

———•———

A month or two after leaving Julian the second time, a regular client, a multimillionaire businessman, invited me to spend some time with him in his third or fourth (who's counting?) vacation home in Pompano Beach, Florida. This forty-something balding man with piercing blue eyes knew what my pimp had done to me. He had seen some of the faded bruises and noticed when I couldn't fake the pain of the broken but healing ribs. He wanted me to go to Florida with him so he could take care of me. The offer was appealing, but this wasn't my Prince Charming, not even one in waiting. I wasn't attracted to him. But I did end up saying yes.

I felt safe around him, protected. He was a sweet man with a messiah complex. I believed he genuinely wanted to see me well. I was so desperate to be loved, anything felt good in that moment. I needed the attention, the feeling of being taken care of by a daddy figure.

So I stayed in this man's beautiful oceanfront condo for a few weeks. It was the first time in years I was able to take a breath, to relax without fear, paranoia, or having to watch my back. I stretched out on a beach, the sand a mere step away from the patio's French doors, and bathed in warm sunlight while inhaling the salty and sweet tropical air. The change of pace, the quiet, was cathartic. At night I dressed in stunning designer little black dresses, and he and I dined in five-star restaurants, gorging on gourmet meals and sipping on five-hundred-dollar bottles of champagne. I came back from the trip refreshed. I felt physically better and was anxious to get back to work to continue saving up money to get out of the life.

The night I got back to Las Vegas, I took a drive to get some food and pulled into an unusually drowsy part of town to fill up my gas tank. I was wearing cut-off shorts and a Hard Rock Café T-shirt my client had bought me in Florida. As I drifted off in my mind for a bit, remembering the cool spray of the ocean on my legs during my morning walks on the beach, I heard the sound of screeching tires. It was a sound I knew all too well. A lump formed in my throat. I didn't even have a few seconds time to reach into my glove compartment and pull out my pearl-handed .25 handgun that I had purchased after I left Julian the second time. All of a sudden I saw Julian's friend's Benz swing around the side of my car.

Déjà vu.

My ex-pimp jumped out of the passenger side holding a pair of large black binoculars, which he slammed down on my head. *Lights out.* The next thing I remember was waking up in the backseat of the car, Julian on top of me giving me one of his signature beatdowns. A pimp friend of his was driving the car and kept yelling, "Yo, man, take it easy. You're getting my seats dirty with blood." The warning didn't make a difference. On the contrary, seeing blood splatter on the white leather fueled Julian's rage. The blows, the scratches, the choking—they all rained down harder.

This is it. I'm going to die tonight.

As Julian screamed words of contempt and disgust at me amidst the flurry of fists, we pulled up to a sprawling home in the suburbs of Las Vegas. He dragged me out of the car by my hair, my face practically being skinned by the cobblestone driveway.

Once inside, he tossed me like a rag doll in the middle of a handful of pimps and their girls, purposely causing a spectacle. On my hands and knees, swallowing the vomit that was coming up my throat, Julian kicked me in the ribs, causing me to collapse and slam my head on the stone tile floor. I knew what he was doing. He was making an example out of me, showing the other girls who were meandering around the entryway and living room in their spiked heels and tight dresses what would happen to them if they left. The other pimps rallied around Julian, egging him on and pointing at me like I was trash dumped out from a garbage can. I heard one of them say to his girl, "Can you believe she had the nerve to run?" Then someone added fuel to the fire and yelled, "And, Julian, she even bought a new car behind your back!"

The beating only got worse. I was, as they called it in the pimp game, "getting served." I lay on the floor writhing in pain while Julian bellowed with a guttural cry for everyone to watch. "This is what's going to happen to you!" he growled, pointing at the girls who by this point were scared out of their minds. Unable to watch, they were staring at the floor, full of fear. Some of them were silently crying, tears dripping down their makeup-smeared faces. But they had no choice. Threatened by Julian and guarded by their pimps, the girls were commanded to watch the bloody scene. (Side note: Years later, on separate occasions, one of the girls and three of the pimps apologized for not doing anything to stop the beating, admitting they had been haunted by the memory for a long time.)

"Take all your clothes off," Julian demanded. I slowly and painfully stripped out of my shorts, T-shirt, and undergarments . . . everything. "Now stand up!" he hissed.

I barely could and almost fell back down on the floor. The shame of being beaten in front of others matched the shame of standing there naked, bare, a sick show of black and blues and torn flesh. Being nude in front of the other pimps was absolutely humiliating. Julian forced me to kneel in front of him and said, "Bend over!" as he reached in his pocket for a pair of hair clippers. My heart sank as the buzzing sound purred in my ears. My long and luscious blond mane was my pride and joy, desired by most in my industry. This was another method of shaming. Julian roughly placed the loud, vibrating machine to my head and started cutting my hair. With my left eye swollen shut, I could barely make out the wisps of blond locks that tore through the air in every direction as tears rained down my face.

The minute the buzzing stopped, Julian got up and grabbed an iron poker by the fireplace. I moaned and spat out blood, another puddle of red to color the stark-white décor. The stench of my own sweat engulfed my nostrils as I stared at the heavy metal object lying threateningly in the palm of his hand.

Julian roared like a maniac when he lifted the iron poker high above his head. I tried to crawl out of the way but it was impossible. With all his might, he used the fireplace accessory to whack me on the leg like a baseball bat. The pain was unbearable. It felt like a grenade exploded in my thigh. I didn't know it at the time, but the blow caused the muscle in my thigh to rupture in half. It didn't take long for my leg from the top of my hip to my knee to turn black from the trauma. The background voices of the pimps got louder. "Hit her harder!" they called out. "She is renegading on you, disrespecting your pimpin'."

As I groaned and writhed on the floor in pain, Julian tossed the iron poker aside and whipped out his Glock. Waving it in the air like a madman, he hissed, "Today is the day you die! I'm gonna shoot you, take you to the desert, and bury you! Who do you think you are, trying to run from me? I'm going to make an example out of you!"

As horrifying as this was, I still was terrified by what the next level of torture would consist of. Before I left Julian, I knew the stories of the other girls I was friends with who had pimps, horrible stories of them "serving them" or "keeping them in line." One of my friends, Cherry, was beat down to the ground, then forced to eat a hard-shell taco that her pimp had defecated on as punishment for drinking while working the escort services. My other girlfriend, Ceceil, was repeatedly sodomized with a broom as she was forced to lay on her knees in a bathtub full of ice.

(Still wondering why working girls stay with their pimps?)

The beatings and berating lasted well into the night. By the time daylight peered in the windows, Julian put his gun to my head and made me get back in the car, bringing with him a girl who had watched the bloody scene. I didn't know it at the time, but Julian had moved this girl and others into my townhouse while I was gone. He made her put on my silk pajamas and sit on the bed while I knelt before her.

The girl sat on my bed, full of fear and panic. Julian roughly grabbed my face with one hand and told the girl, "Look at her! Look at my bottom girl." I can't even imagine what was going through her mind as she was forced to look at me, blood running down my nose, face swollen, black-and-blue eyes stuck shut from caked blood, and a gaping wound with clots of blood on the side of my head where I took the blow of the binoculars. She had to have been terrified. The entire scene was gut-wrenching, and my heart sank, realizing my freedom, the money—*my* money I had been making on my own—it was all over.

Finally, Julian walked me to the spare bedroom as I struggled to gain my footing, pain shooting throughout my body. "Lie down on the bed!" he growled with the gun pointed at my face. I eased my way into the bed, the soft pale-pink sheets stained by dripping blood. Julian fell asleep beside me, his arms crossed on his chest, a finger on the trigger of the gun still pointed my way. The minute I heard him snoring, I got up and limped my way slowly and softly downstairs. I walked into the barely used kitchen, spanking clean, and made a lot noise, pretending I was doing something other than planning my escape. I ran the dishwasher, took out a pot and a package of noodles as if I were going to make something to eat, right before I limped out the side kitchen door to the next townhouse. I'd never met my neighbors, but I was about to, under the worst of circumstances.

My heart pounded wildly in my chest as I rang the doorbell, praying someone would answer. My body trembled as a preppy couple in their early twenties answered the door, their eyes wide in shock as they took one look at this ragged, bludgeoned mess standing before them. I didn't give them a second to say anything and immediately began rambling, talking so fast my words jumped over each other. "Please, please, please," I begged, wiping away tears. "I got kidnapped and beat by my pimp. Can you please drive me to my friend's house?"

Eyes bulging, they stood there for the longest ten or fifteen seconds of my life and then quickly ushered me inside their home. I'll never forget their kindness. This couple gave me ice for my black eyes and face so swollen my nose had disappeared in the swelling. They offered to call the police, which I begged them not to. Again, I was no snitch. And I was also extremely frightened. I made them stick me in the trunk of their car, which was parked in the garage, so Julian wouldn't see and shoot them or me, and they drove me to a side street where I met my friend.

A few days later I was hiding out from Julian while visiting my friend's place at the Budget Suites behind the Stardust Hotel. I couldn't work because the bruising and swelling was the very worst Julian had ever inflicted on me; my face looked like Frankenstein's monster. Someone had tipped Julian off that I was there, and he came by looking for me. All I heard were heavy footsteps behind me as I stood in the parking lot. I knew it was Julian. Clutching the gun I pulled out of my purse, I ran to the front desk. "Call 911!" I yelled as I leapt over the counter to hide. I'm sure the front desk people thought I was a lunatic, but I didn't care. I was scared to death, afraid Julian was here to finally finish me off.

Prostitution vice cops Bill Young and David Logue showed up in ten minutes and arrested Julian. Bill Young, the head of the vice department, and David knew me from my arrests. In fact, Bill was the very first vice cop who arrested me for prostitution. He would later become the sheriff of Las Vegas. He had a soft spot in his heart for me and begged me to get out of the life because he was sure I would die. With tears in his eyes, he pleaded, "Go somewhere, go home, Annie. Just get out of Vegas for a while. You have to get out of this lifestyle. I don't want the next time I see you to be in a body bag."

But where would I go? Even if I went back home to Minneapolis, I'd still live in fear because that was Julian's home as well. I was scared to death. And confused. It was awful.

As soon as Julian got out of jail, my phone burned up. He left the typical messages every day while I nursed myself back to health at my friend's house and eventually got well enough to get back to work. I had to start making up for another loss.

———•———

A few months later I finally went back home to visit my family. I hadn't seen them in years, and I missed them and wanted to spend some time with them.

I heard through the grapevine that Julian was visiting his sister. And after leaving countless voice mails on my phone, spouting apology after apology, I was sucked right back into his vortex and decided to call him. He missed me, Julian said. He needed me. He was extremely depressed. He wished I'd never left—he knew he blew it and that it was his fault. If only he was awarded a "second chance." Did I love him enough to give that to him? This time things had changed him—he realized what he had lost by losing me. He said he wanted to be my boyfriend, like in the beginning of our relationship. I still had a small glimmer of hope that he would change. Pathetic, right?

I also had realized after I left our townhouse following the last severe beating with all the pimps egging him on that he had my jewelry (mainly all my diamond and gold custom jewelry that I worked so hard for), and I wanted it back. According to the pimp-ho rules, pimps are supposed to take whatever the prostitute makes or is given by him as a gift in the relationship. No girl is ever supposed to leave with anything. It is a ploy and tactic used to control and manipulate a woman into staying longer in the relationship, because if she stays, she gets to keep her things. In the Vegas streets, there is this prideful attitude that many of the women have, that if you leave and get anything, you are smarter than a pimp and you ran game back on him. The time I left before, I did take jewelry that was already on my fingers with me because he was out of town—plus my bag of clothes. But *none* of the cash. So this ultimately was part of my motive, to get friendly with him again and act like I was going to "choose up" again with him, so that I could get my jewelry back.

I knew I was flirting with danger, but I wanted to establish a relationship with Julian outside of being his ho. I wanted to give him a chance to really be my friend, and maybe a new chance to be my boyfriend. I wanted to know he still loved me. And maybe he had changed; maybe all the beatings I had endured under his iron fist had softened him in any way. I thought I could actually try playing the "girlfriend" role one more time in our relationship, to start off slow and keep the peace, just to see if he really had changed.

I visited Julian at his sister's and spent the night. He was very affectionate, showering me with kisses. Then, just as I had expected, he pulled out the velvet bag where he kept all my custom jewelry. He took out my massive diamond rings one by one and decorated my fingers with them. He also gave me my diamond-faced watch, my diamond earrings, and my gold feather bone necklace collection.

I thought I was in control, but I was being deceived again. Tempted by the potential for more money and more beautiful jewelry, I was drawn back in that evening.

We had sex, but afterward I felt sick to my stomach. I knew my decision was wrong, stupid. I was trapped again. My pride to get back what was mine had put me in a predicament. Yes, I had my jewelry back, but I had put myself in serious harm's way—again. As Julian slept soundly on the sleeper sofa in his sister's basement, I sat in a chair in the corner, in the dark, unable to sleep. I looked out a little window, clutching my churning stomach. It was snowing, white flakes dancing on the already three-foot blanket of snow that covered the ground. I could smell the purity in the snow, feel the loss of innocence, the hope of a life, dreams. A tear that had been waiting to fall trickled down my face. Then another. Then a flood. It was so overdue. It was like a dam had broken in my soul. I cried for all the years I had wasted, for my heart that had been broken, for my naive desperation to hold on to something that was killing me. Oh, what had I done?

The next day Julian was sweet, acting like the boyfriend he once was, and picked us up some ribs for lunch. Inside I felt empty and lost, but I put on a good show on the outside. I was mad at myself—but an anger and disgust rose up in me and overtook my soul with a fierce veracity. I needed to plan my escape for the very last time!

Julian made plans for us to stop by a local after-hours keg party. On the way there, he made a pit stop, picking up an eighteen-year-old girl named Stacy. I knew where this was going. The nausea flared up again, another physical sign that I had to get myself out of this equation for good. We didn't stay long. I almost passed out in the sea of intoxicated partiers, the dizzying music ringing in my ears, the blurred moments I saw Julian hug Stacy a little too long, a little too close.

The three of us drove back to Las Vegas that night. The entire time I felt like banging my head against the window, wondering what had I done. But still I was headstrong and determined. I was too scared to say I didn't want to be part of the game anymore. I was petrified of getting beat down again in front of another girl because then he would blame me for possibly running her off. The fears manifested in my heart as I wondered how foolish I had been. I knew I was going to escape, but I didn't know how or when or where. I just knew it would have to be as soon as possible.

We got a hotel room when we arrived in Sin City. I told Stacy and Julian I was going to take a shower while they unpacked their bags. As I scrubbed off the grime and sweat of being in a car for twenty-plus hours, my tears mixed with the water collecting at my feet. The sound of the shower drowned out my sobs. I was heartbroken. Reconnecting with Julian in Minneapolis was one of the hardest times I've had with him, outside of the beatings. I knew I had to let go. I knew I had to say good-bye to the abuse, the mental manipulations, the heartache. I needed to live, to finally be free from the imprisonment I had been in for years and do what I wanted.

As I toweled off, I heard the rustle of sheets, bodies colliding, and a familiar grunt. I threw the bathroom door wide open and yelled to the half-clothed, mildly panting pair, "Did y'all just have sex?"

Julian looked at me numbly while Stacy kept her head down. "How dare you do that to me, Julian. That is disgusting!" I raged. Julian continued to keep quiet and started getting dressed. Honestly, I'm surprised he didn't beat me that night. I think he knew I'd had enough. Then he took off to prowl the casinos for more work.

Stacy sat on the bed, still looking embarrassed. I was fuming, but I wasn't mad at her. I knew the deal, as offended as I was by their actions. It was part of the game, the life, *my* life. And it was high time to cut ties.

For the next few weeks, I faked my loyalty while stashing some cash. Julian had promised me he was going to buy a house with the earnings I gave him. He ended up spending the money on a gold BMW 750i. Some habits die hard. During that time, Stacy and I talked about me leaving and making a getaway. I knew I could trust her.

"I gotta go," I told her bluntly one day. "There's no future here for me." I tried to talk her into leaving with me, but she refused. "Fallen, I can't, I care about him," she explained. "I'm not ready to leave yet. Besides, if we both go, he'll definitely hunt us down. If you leave, I can distract him. I can make money to appease him." Stacy promised she would make up the cash from my absence and do whatever it took to get his mind off of me. I knew deep down inside she wasn't going to snitch on me. In all reality, that girl possibly saved my life by staying behind when I left.

That time I left for good—and I never went back. Game over.

CHAPTER 7

RENEGADE

Renegade: a person who leaves one group, religion, etc.,
and joins another that opposes it.
—Merriam-Webster.com

I went back to my routine of working days after leaving Julian for the last time. I needed to work just to pay the bills, pouring on the heavy charm when the hotel door closed behind me. I hustled with sweet and seductive words, devouring the crisp bills men put in my hand, one after another, so we could both get a fix. No longer a way to earn the love I so desperately wanted and needed, I worked just to make money, the tool that would help me gain my independence, what I hoped would eventually be a square life.

I was in my twenties, young and pretty, but it seemed the best years of my life were passing me by. I felt old, tired, broken down. I needed an escape, a way to soothe the deep wounds left behind by a failed relationship and to numb the overwhelming fear that the pimp mafia would one day find me and kill me.

The first five years of living in Las Vegas were, for the most part, absent of partying and drinking. All that changed, ever so slowly, when I permanently cut ties with Julian. Besides, not working every single day gave me a cushion of time I never had, margin to let my hair down and let loose. I finally had friends, fellow renegade call girls like myself whom I met through the escort agency.

My friends were gorgeous and good-hearted. Karen was a petite and sassy long-haired blonde who got started, like me, walking the track in Hawaii. Deena looked like Cleopatra with her strong Egyptian features of high cheekbones and dreamy brown eyes. Katrina was a sharp-tongued, blue-eyed, curvy blonde, and Cinnamon was a stunning, tall, light-skinned African American who was like a chameleon, blending into any environment, whether she was hobnobbing with the elite or hanging out in the hood. I loved these girls. And they loved me. We hung out, shopped, shot back rum and Cokes at swanky bars and hot dance clubs, and passionately trash-talked possessive men and pimps who marked their territory by treating women as objects and slaves.

Here's the thing about these girls. On one hand, they were renegades like me, independent escorts, but most of them had boyfriends to whom they gave a part of their earnings. Keep in mind, they weren't expected to hand over every single dollar they made; it was their choice to give financially what they wanted, on their own terms. A part of me was jealous because they had the kind of relationships with their boyfriends that I had struggled so hard, and so unsuccessfully, to create with Julian. They were tough, strong women who knew the game but broke the rules, toying much too close with danger.

I saved up about $14,000 in a few months after leaving Julian, who continued to call and follow me around. I saw him a few times after I finally left for good, once at a stoplight by the escort agency where he pulled out his gun and pointed it at me. I immediately ran about five red lights on the Las Vegas Strip to get away from him. He was waving the gun at me and yelling obscenities as he chased me through the lights. I finally pulled into a parking garage and hid on the bottom floor, hoping I had given him the slip—I had, and he didn't find me.

Then one night I was at a famous nightclub called Sharks when he spotted me coming to meet my girlfriends for a drink. He pulled me to the back door of the club (in front of the bouncers) and proceeded to bash my face out by the palm trees and garden, yelling that I was disrespecting the game by coming into the club as a renegade and showing my face to all the hoes with pimps.

Eventually, after a long time of avoiding him, he dropped out of the picture for good. I got my own place, a luxurious apartment right off the Strip. Soon after, I bought a convertible Mustang with a white leather interior and twelve-inch woofers, dropping about seven grand a few weeks later on a candy-apple-green custom paint job. Work thrived with high-roller clients. When I needed to pay bills, the money flowed.

I met Jack on a call from the agency. A short guy with long blond hair, he was born in Scotland. Though he lived in the States most of his life, his tongue betrayed him sometimes with the slightest hint of a Scottish accent. I thought it was charming. Jack had booked a spacious suite at Bally's, where he and five or six of his buddies, mellow dudes in their mid-twenties to early thirties, partied hard. I took the call with a few girlfriends of mine from the agency. My fellow working girls and I were in good spirits, strolling down the carpeted hallway, walls papered in deep gold and decorated with black-and-white portraitures displaying Hollywood icons such as Humphrey Bogart and Frank Sinatra.

When we arrived, I curiously noted a brown paper lunch bag on a side table, toppled on its side with stacks of cash spilling out. I quoted him a thousand dollars for the hour. Jack smiled politely and reached into a nearby desk to pull out the first grand. More cash was stocked inside. A lot more. I noticed the bills were tinged purple. *Odd.*

Jack and I exchanged small talk, lounging on the plush couch with the backdrop of the dazzling Strip behind us. His buddies whipped out bottles of champagne from the stocked bar and indulged with the other girls. A cacophony of clinking glasses, laughter, and frolic doused their air. Jack was sweet but glum. He had just broken up with a Playboy playmate girlfriend and was heartbroken. His broken spirit was palpable.

We spent a few hours together, ordering room service and dining on filet mignon and rock lobster. Jack wanted to gamble, though, and he stuffed his designer jeans' pockets with wads of cash before we moved our party to the casino below, spending most of the money at a blackjack table. He won several bets, commenting I was his lucky charm, and slid me a five-thousand-dollar chip as a token of his appreciation. As the night wore on, and Jack pounded back more rum and Cokes, his quiet, in-control demeanor started slipping. Speech slurred, eyes bloodshot, he took me back to his suite. Unable to perform, he paid me for the night and we parted ways. It was a good day at work.

Jack called the agency the next day and asked for me. This time we were alone. We dined at an expensive French restaurant and talked. He was inquisitive, peppering me with questions, personal ones. I told him my story, about growing up, the sexual abuse, my dad, my pimp, the physical abuse. He was compassionate in response, listening intently, reaching his hand out toward mine in the warm glow of candlelight. That night he talked more about his ex-girlfriend and told me he owned a successful jewelry piercing distribution company. Similar to the night before, the date ended with a warm hug, no sex.

More calls followed. Jack liked me, and he didn't hold back in telling me so. While I didn't reciprocate the feelings, he was kind and fun to be around. I felt safe, a feeling I appreciated and longed for. But Jack wasn't all roses and fairy tales. I quickly noticed he was rarely sober. He popped Valium like they were Tic Tacs and liked his liquor just as much. "It takes the edge off," he'd say about the white pills, gulping down a few with a swash of whiskey, a habit I became accustomed to.

A month after we met, he flew me first class to Los Angeles. We stayed at the beautiful Lowe's Santa Monica Beach Hotel with its breathtaking view of the ocean. We took scenic drives in his brand-new Corvette, speeding down the Pacific Coast Highway with the breeze blowing through my hair. He drove a little too fast for my taste. The one time he whipped a turn close to eighty miles an hour, I practically slammed into the driver's seat. "Don't you ever do that again!" I yelled, my heart pounding wildly in my chest, to which he yelled back something about me needing to relax or take a Valium or something. The five-minute argument we had about speed was the only time we fought. Jack was laid-back; he didn't have an aggressive bone in his body. We spent the next two days hanging out at pool parties hosted in sprawling mansions in the Hollywood Hills and soaking in the sun on crystalline Pacific beaches.

Our conversations were the same. Jack would try to persuade me to leave the business. "I'll take care of you for the rest of your life," he promised. "What is it going to take for you to get out?" I appreciated the kind offer, but I could never take him up on it. He was a nice guy, young, successful, well-connected, rich—all the things that looked good on paper. While Jack wasn't just a client, and was fast becoming a friend, I wasn't attracted to him. I didn't want to establish a romantic relationship with him and started to feel bad about it, especially when he told me he loved me and wanted to spend more time with me. "I can't fake my feelings," I told him matter-of-factly before I reminded him of my daily rate. It sounds cold, but it was part of the job. There were terms to our agreement. Jack didn't hire me to fall in love.

Once in a while, guilt would hit me pretty hard. A part of me almost wanted to like him, hoping he could be my knight in shining armor who would whisk me away on his white horse. But the fact was, I didn't share his sentiment. Besides, the guy was a mess. Jack's addiction teetered on a thin, self-destructive ledge. During one of our talks, which I ended to the tune of "it's not you, it's me," he broke down. We were in the hotel room when he grabbed a brown bottle of Valium, the sound echoing like maracas, and threatened, "If you're not going to love me, I'm going to just kill myself!" He flung the cap off the bottle and threw it across the room as he lifted a handful of pills to his mouth.

"Jack, no—" I screamed, lunging toward him with my arm outstretched. I managed to knock the pills out of his hand, scattering them like seeds on the floor. "What are you doing?" I cried out. I knew he was hurting. I knew he was broken. I felt sorry for him, but I couldn't fix him. Heck, I didn't even know how to fix myself.

Jack calmed down, gazing out the window as the sea stretched through the soft horizon, waves lapping on a practically empty shoreline dotted with canopied cabanas. "There's no point in living," he whispered. Then turning his head sharply toward me, he stared into my eyes with a firm, yet quiet voice and said, "I've been a very bad person. I've done bad things. And I feel terrible about it." Silence followed. I didn't know what to say, so I kept my mouth shut and held his hand instead. We talked for a bit before he became lethargic and dozed off for the evening while I flipped through hundreds of TV channels on a big screen watching nothing in particular. I left for Vegas the following morning, kissing Jack on the cheek.

A few weeks later my cell phone rang as I was speeding through a lucky string of yellow lights. "Is this Annie Lobert?" asked a male voice, stern and professional. I got scared. Nobody called me Annie anymore. I was adamant about being called Fallen, my call girl name. And the guy suspiciously sounded like a cop. I'd been around them enough to tell.

"Can I help you?" I vaguely answered, not denying or admitting my identity.

The man introduced himself as an FBI agent. "I'd like to meet with you at the Pepper Mill. I'm working on the case of a person of interest that I have evidence of your involvement with. You can either cooperate and talk to me or risk getting indicted or arrested."

I started panicking. My hands were sweating all over the steering wheel, and I had to pull over to finish the conversation. My mind raced. Was it Julian? Did something happen? I racked my brain trying to figure out who I knew that could be in trouble with the FBI. Other than pimps I had known, courtesy of my ex, my search came up empty. Maybe it was a trick, a scheme.

Despite some reservation, I took the bait and made my way to the Pepper Mill, a local restaurant. I scanned the busy joint, packed with sunburned tourists and locals, when a man in a dark suit stood up and motioned me his way.

Bruce was pleasant, nonthreatening. And he really was an FBI agent, discreetly showing me his badge. In fact, he was the head of the Nevada FBI! He told me he had me on video camera with a man the agency was investigating. Sliding a black-and-white picture of me sitting at a casino playing table, he asked, "Do you recognize this man?" and pointed to the young, long-haired guy sitting next to me in the photograph, behind tall stacks of chips.

I nodded. It was Jack.

Bruce asked me how I knew him, giving me incentive to talk by stating he had more videos and photographs of us together that confirmed an obvious connection. I blanked for a second while he continued to talk. I wasn't about to tell him I was a prostitute, but I couldn't escape the evidence that I was somehow connected with Jack. "This man is part of a string of eight bank robberies in LA," Bruce said, much to my shock. Apparently Jack and his buddies had entered the banks by blowing up holes through the roof or the walls before the start of business.

He paused for a moment, allowing the information to sink in. "Annie, did you ever notice the color of the money he had?" My mind flashed back to the purple dye on the stacks of bills Jack had given me. The sign of stolen cash! How could I have overlooked that? Bruce continued, telling me that Jack was in the middle of entering a plea deal. He could either go to jail for twenty years or snitch on his friends and enter the witness protection program. "So, what can you tell us about Jack? How do you know him?"

I didn't know what to say. I didn't know what I could say other than the truth. "I'm a high-class call girl," I admitted. Bruce quickly realized I didn't have any involvement in the crimes. He expressed his concern for Jack and that he was uneasy about his safety, especially in light of his violent accomplices he was likely going to rat out. I met with the FBI agent one more time. To my surprise, Jack joined us. We spoke for a while. Jack was quiet, nervous, saying good-bye and telling me he had always loved me. That was the last time I saw him.

Bruce called me years later. "I have bad news, Annie. Jack finally did it. He took his own life." My heart sank. I knew Jack was a troubled soul. And I knew he had suicidal tendencies. But the reality of him killing himself still shook me to my core. I thought of the jewelry he bought me, ruby and diamond rings. He was always trying to buy my love, the same way I tried to buy Julian's. It didn't work. It never works. Love can never be bought.

Though I serviced men in different capacities for a living, I still longed for companionship, for a genuine connection. With Julian out of the picture, life was lonely. In many ways, with the financial freedom I finally had and being able to party at hot spots, life was fun, but I felt empty without a man.

I hate to say this, but men were my fix, my high. I've always loved being in relationships, having someone to come home to, to talk to, to look forward spending time with. Slipping in through my front door in the morning after work, yawning with heels in hand, I wasn't thrilled being greeted by the quiet. As sunlight poured in through the many skylights that brightened the place, I'd crawl into bed. Alone. I didn't like that feeling. Not one bit. Because it was causing me to face who I was and what I was doing for a living. It was shameful and depressing. I was an empty girl trying to find my purpose.

So when I was out at a club one night with my girlfriends and my eyes landed on a gorgeous man who was turning out quite a show with his fierce dance moves, I fell hard. Big surprise. Peter and I hooked up that night and started dating. It was also good for my image on the Las Vegas Strip to have a public romantic interest, because I could use him as a front to other pimps, appearing that I "chose up" with another pimp so they would stop harassing me. Peter knew I was against pimps and was aware of what I had just lived through. Life and love—all of it was always in the fast lane for me. At first Peter was sweet, charming, kind. He didn't show any signs of violent or abusive behavior . . . until later in our relationship.

Peter was a jealous man, particularly after his nightly ritual of virtually drowning himself in malt liquor. Name-calling and accusations would fly out of his mouth. I never admitted to Peter what I did for a living, hiding behind the lie of being a stripper who did stripper grams. I don't think he ever believed me, though; he would always search my purse to find condoms. We fought constantly. Peter would accuse me of lying, of being a whore. He convinced me to buy bars for the windows of our house and had a sick habit of locking me inside like a prisoner when he was angry at me. He even lived off my money after he lost his job and was out of work for so long. The entire relationship, which would last about four years, was another toxic mess.

Sometime in 1994, I headed to Italy for a few months with a friend who was part of a traveling theatre troupe. I remember being startled as soon as I stepped off the plane, still slightly disoriented from the long and bumpy flight. As a woman's voice echoed over the loudspeaker in Italian ushering passengers through the terminal to their gates, I looked around the international hub with a mixture of awe and confusion. Almost immediately, my eyes fell on soldiers in military fatigues strolling around, eyes wandering. They had what I believe were M-16 assault rifles slung over their shoulders, as naturally as if they were toting backpacks. While the sight unarmed me, one of my Italian friends later assured me it was normal; soldiers frequently patrolled the area, and their presence didn't necessarily indicate danger lurking around the corner.

Thanks to my friend, I tagged along with the thirty-plus people troupe traveling through the western region of Lazio, through provinces like Frosinone, Latina, and my personal favorite, Rome, in a caravan of trailers that housed our sleeping quarters and the staging, lighting, and other equipment needed to set up and tear down the show. I loved Italy, the people, the food, the smells, their positive outlook on life. The Italian culture was relaxed, unlike the fast-paced hustle I was used to in the States. The Italians took time to enjoy their day and each other. Every day around lunchtime, stores would shut down and the cities were virtually quiet, the absence of loud and animated conversations making the scene almost uncomfortably silent. Italy was beautiful, and outside of my continual wonder of the stunning countryside rolling with olive and lemon trees and the medieval hilltop villages colored by magnificent green gardens overlooking the Black Sea, I was struck by the spiritual history of the place.

I had packed my Gideon Bible with me, the same one my musician friend had used to show me the powerful love of Jesus through its redemptive stories. I don't know why I took it, I just did. I kept that red hard-covered book close throughout the years, tucked safely in different nightstands. Not that I would pull it out and devour the words on the thin pages; it was just comforting to know the Book was there. On the way to Rome, I read the entire New Testament for the first time in years, carefully breaking in the stiff spine and flipping through the crisp and very noisy pages.

As I read the New Testament, I was touched deeply and realized that I was the prodigal daughter who needed to come home. I cried through the hours it took me to read it. It awakened something dormant—the goodness God had already put in me was confirmed by the stories of the women who followed Him and served Him . . . that I could be one of them . . . that I could choose to do the right thing finally. It changed me forever.

During the days we spent traveling, slowly climbing dusty mountain roads and dangerously weaving through chaotic city traffic, I lay on the cramped bunk bed in the trailer reading the Gospels. I read about Peter and his tendency to talk first and think later. I read about the woman caught in the act of adultery and how Jesus sent away her condemners through a cryptic message He traced in the desert sand. I read about the apostle Paul and how his miraculous conversion led him from killing Christians to leading them. I cried as I read those beautiful stories and words. For the first time I was awakened to

God's Word. I had never before realized how powerful it was. The Scriptures did something to my soul. Something shifted inside. I knew I had to get out of prostitution, but I just didn't know how. The prodigal daughter needed to start her journey of walking home.

And as I read, I prayed. I thought about the trajectory of my life, the toxic relationship I had escaped, the current one that entrapped me, the emptiness in my soul that no man, no amount of money, and no expensive outfit could fill. "God, please help me" would become my signature prayer. Few words, but packed with more meaning than I could ever explain. Sometimes the best prayers are the shortest, absent of meaningless or trite phrases that aim to impress, but rather bursting with desperation birthed from shadows and dark places.

My Italian friends had prepared me for our stop in Rome by describing the Vatican, the Holy City, not just with reverent reflection, but also with a spirit of passion, a deep respect and love for their faith. I admired their devotion, and though I didn't understand the particulars of their beliefs, I knew it was real. I had a sense God was present on this trip and talking to me through what would be a spiritual epiphany.

When I walked the Vatican grounds, I couldn't stop crying. Words were hard to come by when I stood inside St. Peter's Basilica. I felt so small standing in one of the largest churches in the world, marveling at the intricately laden and breathtaking artwork, colossal sculptures, and exquisite and unmatched workmanship. Charles Dickens described the iconic church's unmatched beauty best: "The first burst of the interior, in all its expansive majesty and glory: and, most of all, the looking up into the Dome; is a sensation never to be forgotten."

Time stopped when I stood in front of Michelangelo's beautiful Pietà, the sculpture of the grieved Virgin Mary cradling her dead son, Jesus, after He was crucified. I felt God's presence shroud me like a warm blanket, cradling my wounds, my pain, my terrible sin. I felt humbled that day, as the reality of my line of work deeply stung my conscience. Walking among the gushing tourists whose eyes swept slowly across every inch of this magnificent place, I whispered under my breath, "God, can You please get me out of this life? I can't do this anymore. I want to come home." I had no desire to get religious and become a Bible thumper, but I sensed a spiritual awakening of sorts, a covering of grace that Jesus was real, close, extending a hand of love.

I visited the Coliseum later that day with my Italian friends, who told me about the Christians who were martyred there, their innocent blood spilled in this ancient epicenter of Roman entertainment. I placed my hand on the centuries-old limestone, oblivious to the obnoxiously loud tour guides around me and the masses that followed. I was struck by the thought of my fellow brothers and sisters before me who had died in that place. I felt heat emanate from the aged wall. I can only say it was a holy moment, one that captured the presence of God, not just around me, but also in me.

I left Italy feeling hopeful, even though I was going home to a life that radically betrayed my fairy-tale dreams. I prayed on the plane, wrestling with the sickening feeling in the pit of my stomach when I thought about my love life, the toxic man I was involved with. "I'm going back to the States, God," I prayed silently as I leaned back in my seat, "but I need Your help. I don't want to do this anymore."

Despite the real feeling that God was pursuing me, I started partying harder when I returned home, numbing my layered pain with alcohol. I felt extremely guilty for having to go back to work in order to survive and began to plan my escape after having experienced the presence of God on a deep level that was so tangible. I knew I had to figure out how I was going to take the first steps to attempt fleeing my captor because I was again trapped in an extremely abusive relationship. I was lying in bed alone that summer afternoon in 1995, slowly awakening after working all night, when I noticed a few dime-sized lumps on the right side of my neck. I made an appointment with a nearby ears, nose, and throat specialist who biopsied the swollen nodules, and a few days later he gave me a clean bill of health, assuring me nothing was wrong.

A month later I started experiencing intense itching on my elbows, ankles, legs, and hands. I scratched day and night, so hard that my nails dug into the skin and rashes formed. I hit every pharmacy, plunking down hundreds of dollars on different creams and ointments. Nothing worked. I settled on guzzling liquid Benadryl as if it were water, the only remedy that offered the slightest bit of relief. Then I noticed more lumps than before, and bigger in size. In a few days, my neck swelled like a balloon, and I immediately scheduled another biopsy. This time I wasn't in the clear.

It was a typical September afternoon when a nurse from my doctor's office phoned me and without emotion said, "Annie, the results came back. The lumps in your neck are tumors and the biopsy confirmed Hodgkin's lymphoma, cancer of the lymph nodes. The itching you've been experiencing is also a symptom." The nurse then shared my cancer was in Stage 2B, advanced yet treatable.

Cancer. The room started spinning. I found it almost impossible to keep the phone steady in my shaking hands.

"We need to get you in the office and schedule you for laparoscopic surgery to determine if the cancer has reached your organs." Emotions swirled like the chaotic art of a child's fingerpaint creation. All sorts of thoughts collided into one another.

It is my fault.

I am a bad girl.

God is angry with me.

I deserve this.

God is punishing me for my lifestyle.

It's too late to leave. I will die here, trapped.

I hung up the phone in a strange marriage of disbelief and devastation. And I was annoyed too. Hearing that I had cancer over the telephone and not face-to-face made me feel like a specimen, not a human being. That night I crawled into bed, feeling defeated. I tossed and turned, unable to process the wretched phone call. I felt alone, betrayed by God, and guilty because of my choices.

About a week later, my boyfriend drove me to the hospital where I was scheduled for laparoscopic surgery. No one said a word. Full of fear, I didn't know what to expect, still struggling with my fluctuating emotions. I prayed as I stared out the window, sunglasses shading my eyes that burned with tears. "God, please help, help me get better." It was the only prayer I knew how to pray. What else was there to say?

Upon being wheeling out of the recovery room, I learned that there had been clusters of tumors in my neck and several in my lungs. The surgeons also had to remove my spleen because it was so enlarged. I stayed in the hospital for a week recovering.

I had my first radiation treatment at the clinic on November 9, 1995. I was custom-fitted with a mouth guard to protect my mouth, tongue, and salivary glands from the radiation. I lay in a cradle-type bed in what looked like a giant X-ray machine while it made loud noises and beeps. The technicians encouraged me to relax, to think positive thoughts, and to find my happy place. As I lay feeling somewhat claustrophobic in a spaceship-like contraption, I couldn't even begin to imagine how to relax. Then there was that horrid smell. As red beams of light radiated the cancerous cells in my body, honing in on the permanent purple dot tattoos the doctor had marked on my skin, the odor of burnt flesh wafted around me. I had been warned not to move, to lie as still as possible, so the radiating beams wouldn't hit my spine and possibly leave me paralyzed. Every few minutes the radiation therapist in the adjoining room would ask through an intercom system how I was doing. *Just peachy, thanks.*

As the machine whirred like a vacuum cleaner, I closed my eyes tight and prayed, "God, please help me. Heal me. Help." It didn't make sense at the time, but even though I was scared and unsure and angry and depressed and devastated and all of those things, I felt God's presence. I felt His love and peace. I felt hopeful. Odd, isn't it? Hopeful, even while high-energy rays worked to kill cancer cells with laser focus.

My treatment would consist of radiation every day, five days a week, until January 31, 1996. I had a break after a few months and then another cycle of treatments. My hair started falling out in a straight line where the radiation hit, from one ear to the other. It looked like I had a reverse bowl haircut. The entire right side of my neck became an ulcerated sore, which I had to bandage daily because it constantly oozed pus. I covered the wound with a scarf so no one would notice, particularly my tricks. I worked sporadically during this time, when I had the energy and wasn't throwing up for hours at a time. While a couple of the phone girls from the agency were supportive and regularly checked on me, Peter continued to be abusive and call me all kinds of terrible names, even ridiculing me for my cancer.

The relationship was trying, and though I wanted to leave him, I couldn't because I was so sick. Where would I go? Who would take me to all my radiation treatments and doctors' appointments? Would I die because of the disruption in my schedule for cancer treatments if I left him and had to find a new place to live? My only option was to stay and suck it up. Once again I was trapped in a terrible relationship. It was a little different from the one I had been in with Julian. Although Peter didn't like my job, he knew I had to work, and he lived off of me and completely controlled my every move. I strategically planned my escape behind his back, however. I knew how violent he was and feared the many times he threatened me with his gun would one day become more than a threat. I had to be careful.

CHAPTER 8

GLORIOUS DISASTER

*"Our lives in Christ are like rays that continually expand
and extend from that one stunning moment when his
glorious light overtook our darkness."*
—Lisa Bevere

On December 6, 1995, my brother Chuck called. "Diane had a heart attack," he said, choking back tears. My heart went to the pit of my stomach. "No, God. Not this."

I left for Minneapolis that night. The three-hour flight seemed to take forever. Despite being weak from radiation treatments, I couldn't sleep. Placing my head uncomfortably on the side of the window, I stared out at the plane's wing as it hovered over the bright lights of Vegas, a city just beginning to stretch out her arms and rouse for a party-filled night.

The city quickly dimmed to a blur as my thoughts nestled on my sister, whom I had kept in touch with over the years but had only seen on a handful of occasions. Diane, only thirty-one years old, had a good life. She was married to a great guy and loved her job at IDS, the company I had worked for after high school. She knew I was in a toxic relationship and had begged me to leave. Diane was always worried for me, loving me well in her nonthreatening and nonjudgmental way.

When I arrived at the hospital, the mood was grim. Bill and Chuck were there, as well as my parents. I hugged them all, resting in my mother's arms a little longer than I had in the others'. Diane's prognosis wasn't good. The doctors didn't even try to offer hope.

I learned the details of what had happened talking to my parents, concerned nurses, and doctors working hard to salvage whatever life they could. Diane was giving a presentation at work when she had a heart attack. My friend Michelle, who also worked at IDS, told me more heartbreaking details. While my sister was collapsed on the floor, gasping for air, her co-workers stood by, doing nothing. Nobody would touch her, let alone give her CPR, because of her severe buckteeth. It broke my heart that not one person had the decency to look past the abnormality to help. While some of her co-workers did call 911, no one was able to get through. A new telephone system had been implemented and outgoing calls to the emergency line were met with silence. (Most people didn't carry cell phones in the mid-nineties.) By the time paramedics were able to reach her, Diane had been without oxygen for twenty minutes. At that point, her brain started to swell and shut down. Once in the hospital, doctors ran a barrage of tests to determine the extent of the damage, but her condition didn't look good. They put her in a drug-induced coma and hooked her up to a ventilator to help her breathe as well as other life support machines.

I sat beside Diane in the hospital, holding her IV-taped hand and speaking softly, telling her doctors were doing their best to get her better. I stared at my sister, her eyes closed, as the ventilator hypnotically beeped and whirred, artificially maintaining her oxygen flow. I had brought with me a portable CD player and placed the headphones on her ears, careful not to interfere with the web of wires and tubes that covered her. A music lover like myself, I played one of her favorite Michael Jackson songs, "You Are Not Alone." I don't know if she could hear it, or hear me singing along with whispered breath. I stroked her arm, wondering if she could feel my touch. Despite knowing she was fully unconscious, I thought that she might just wake up, like you see in the movies. Maybe the song would move her, remind her to open her eyes, remind her body to do what it was supposed to do, breathe. We took turns sitting with Diane while the rest of the family hung out in the ICU waiting room, pacing around nervously in the quiet room that had housed thousands of families before us, some eventually leaving with smiles and prayers of gratitude while others left in tears.

My family didn't speak much during the course of those first few days. We just nodded at each other and exchanged unimportant small talk that awkwardly filled the silence. We were all overwhelmed in our own way by what had happened with Diane, feeling painfully helpless, unsure, uncertain.

As the hours passed, slowly and without resolve, the doctors assured us there was nothing to do except wait. Tests, then more tests, had to be run. I had blown off my radiation treatment to see my sister and was told to go home, finish my round of treatment, and I'd be notified if there was a change in Diane's condition. The medical team working on her would have a better picture of her outlook in a few days.

I wasn't home more than a week when I got a call from the hospital. "Come now," was the word. The team of nurses and doctors were going to start the process of taking my sister off the ventilator. Sadly, it wasn't because her lungs started functioning; it was because recent tests showed she had, at best, 6 percent brain activity. In other words, "Come now so you can say good-bye." I left for Minneapolis that day.

A doctor had removed Diane's breathing tube and inserted a tracheotomy so she could continue to breathe through that tube. No one knew what was going to happen, how long she'd be able to breathe on her own. Next, the nurses began to shut down the machines one by one that were giving Diane fluids and nutrients, sustaining her life. It was another waiting game, except now we knew the outcome; it was only a matter of time.

None of us said much. My mom rarely left Diane's side, cupping her oldest daughter's hand in hers, mumbling a whispered mix of prayers and "I love yous." On December 22, 1995, while we lingered in the ICU waiting room, flipping through the same magazines we had looked through the past two weeks and clasping cups of coffee so our hands could do something, a nurse in baby-blue scrubs rushed into the room. "Everyone, get in Diane's room!" she exclaimed, piercing the quiet room with her shrill cry.

I shuddered. I wasn't ready. How do you say good-bye to your big sister who was also your best friend?

My mom stood on one side of Diane, my dad on the other. I watched my sister from the foot of the bed, with Bill and Diane's husband there as well. Chuck had stepped out of the room to get some air, shaken up by the ordeal.

Diane's eyes were open, and although her body had been shutting down for the past two weeks, she could cough on her own. I stared at my sister, barely alive, knowing this was the last time I would see her. I can't even describe the hole in my heart I felt at her coming absence. As her breathing labored by the minute, she gasped and let out a moan, her last. I believed she cried out knowing she was leaving us all.

While the finality of death was obvious, the room was filled with the presence of peace, like a holy moment that not even death had the power to desecrate.

Hours later, I lay on the living room couch in Diane's house. A week before she had the heart attack, she had put up her Christmas tree, taking time to create a breathtaking presentation of dazzling lights and delicate ornaments that hung with precision, picture perfect in their rightful places. My eyes, blurred with tears, fixed on the lights until sleep came.

I dreamt I was sitting at her country kitchen table, staring out the large picture window at the snow, glimmering like diamonds in the light of the full moon. Then Diane walked in, all smiles.

"Hi, Annie," she exclaimed with a peaceful glow radiating around her. "I went to heaven."

"What's it look like?" I asked, stunned and my heart racing.

"Oh, it's beautiful, Annie. Indescribable!"

"Did you see Jesus?"

"Oh yes!" She nodded excitedly.

My sister looked so happy, even after her smile somewhat faded. "Annie," she said quietly. "I have to go." In the dream,

I looked out the window, and by the time I turned my head to the spot where my sister had stood just seconds earlier, it was empty. Dark. Just like that, Diane was gone.

I abruptly woke up, my palms drenched with sweat. I felt paralyzed. I literally couldn't move. As my heart pounded out of my chest, the lights on the Christmas tree turned off, as did the lamp I had left on before I drifted off to sleep. This wasn't a power outage or a circuit breaker problem. Silence filled the dark room, save for my rapid breaths when I heard the unmistakable sound of footsteps walk through the room. I didn't see anything, but I knew it was Diane. I just knew. I truly believe I was in a supernatural place. Still lying down, unable to even lift myself off the couch, I felt a wave of heat course through my body, from my toes all the way through and stopping for a short time at my neck, where the tumors were. I believed this was a physical turning point for the cancer, that God was supernaturally touching me.

My sister's death changed me in ways good and not so good. While it developed in me a stronger belief in God—I started exploring faith, reading books like *The Bible Code* and others about angels, as well as non-Christian books on the existence of God—at the same time it sent me over the edge. Within a matter of a few months, five people I knew, including my grandfather, passed away. I was engulfed in grief and couldn't help obsessing over my own mortality. I thought I was going to hell. I knew God was a God of mercy, but I was scared, full of fear, and hoping He would give me a chance.

Though I was strong for my family while we made the funeral arrangements and endured the gut-wrenching experience of burying our beloved Diane, I fell apart in Vegas. I needed help. The grief lasted for months, steady and at times explosive. Life was getting to be a bit too much. I needed to get out of the business. But I needed a push. I couldn't break free on my own.

———•———

My last radiation treatment was toward the end of summer of 1996. I didn't feel hopeful; I could still feel lumps on my neck. "Check again," I asked my doctor. "I don't think the cancer is gone."

Blood work and CT and PET scans concluded I had malignant tumors in my neck and spine. Within a week, on September 26, 1996, I was scheduled for my first round of chemotherapy. My doctor warned I was going to get very sick, even worse than I had with the radiation. His words, however, couldn't prepare me for the inevitable.

Once a month for the next year, I trekked to a local outpatient cancer clinic and sat in a room with ten La-Z-Boy chairs occupied by fellow cancer patients at different stages of the disease. A panoramic window overlooked a beautiful garden, giving us a calm view to stare at while doses of chemo coursed through our veins.

As soon as I got home after my first dose of the chemo, I ran to the bathroom. For the next seven hours I had severe diarrhea and threw up until there was nothing left to get out. For the next month, I basically felt like myself at best once a week. Chemo was unbearable, ravaging my body as the drugs attacked the cancer cells. I lost a significant amount of weight, so much that my doctors were worried I'd die from malnourishment. But

I couldn't eat; I felt too sick. Because I was stuck repeatedly with needles during my treatment and for testing, my doctors were concerned that my veins would collapse and implanted a port under my skin on my arm so they could access my veins easily.

My hair started falling out in clumps, and what remained were inch-long strands that were as fine as feathers. I chose not to shave my hair and spent thousands of dollars on beautiful human-haired wigs. After all, I still had to work and, as unbelievable as it seems, I continued working as a high-class call girl as often as possible. Someone had to pay the bills, and I still didn't know how I could ever get a job doing anything different that would pay for my medical bills.

At the end of my chemo treatment I started partying hard, drinking to oblivion with my girlfriends four times a week, many times not remembering what had happened the night before. During the cancer treatments, I had been taking Lorcets on occasion when the pain in my bones and muscles got really bad. I didn't know until later I was allergic to narcotics, however, and my skin was always itchy and covered with rashes from my extreme scratching. The occasional pill popping for pain turned into an addiction, from half a pill a day to four. Though my cancer was in remission (and would ultimately be cured), I was a complete mess on the outside, the inside, and within my spirit as well.

I was angry at God and struggled with a mix of emotions I didn't know how to process. I felt massive guilt and crippling shame from my lifestyle. I felt fear from my cancer diagnosis. I felt grief from my sister's death. I remember driving on Interstate 15 one night, putting pedal to the metal and watching the speedometer reach just past 140 mph. As I roared down the highway I yelled, "Just flip the car, God! Just do it! You took my sister. Why not take me too?"

Though a part of me knew God was real and somehow involved in my life, I couldn't see past the chaos. That incredible experience in Italy seemed so far and distant from my mind and heart, like it was only a dream that I wished had happened. Was God real? Could He see me? Did He even love me? I desperately tried numbing my feelings while grasping for a sliver of hope that change was possible. I fumbled my way through life, continuing to make poor choices, and on April 17, 1998, I tried cocaine for the first time at a girlfriend's birthday party. It was love at first snort. The indescribable high I experienced lasted for eight hours. I felt on top of the world. No problems. No worries. No negative thoughts. No drowning in guilt, fear, or shame. I was euphoric, empowered. For once in my life, I felt invincible. The pressure was finally off by relieving the edge I felt. I got high whenever I could behind Peter's back. It was my new addiction. And it was my one escape that seemed to work every time, no matter what situation I was facing.

Guilt played a huge factor in me staying with Peter as long as I did. I felt sorry for him and the crazy personal problems he had. Although I had been planning to leave him for a long time, even getting another apartment on the sly where I had hoped one day to move into on my own, my boyfriend tried to take care of me, shuffling me to my doctor's appointments and chemo sessions and cooking for me. A part of me is grateful for his presence during one of the worst times of my life. But that doesn't negate the fact that he was abusive and even psychotic.

One day he took out a .357 magnum, one of many in his gun collection, inserted a hollow-point bullet, and spun the chamber.

He had always threatened to kill himself if I ever left. Peter put the gun in my hands and said if I didn't kill him, he would kill me. I stood in the dining room facing this crazy man, shaking in fear. I pointed the gun at him and told him I wasn't going to kill him. "Do it," he yelled, and I pulled the trigger.

I had purposely aimed the gun inches away from where he stood, and the bullet flew through the metal frame in the glass sliding door, eventually resting in a concrete wall in the back of our yard. Peter continued to roar obscenities at me as he walked into the backyard to retrieve the shattered bullet. I was still standing frozen in the dining room when he came back, calm as a cucumber. As he placed the bullet fragments and gun in a Ziploc bag, he said menacingly, "When the police come for you one day, I'm going to have you arrested for attempted murder." You see? He was sick.

I left Peter the next day. My brother Chuck, who was living in Vegas at the time, came with me to the house, along with one of my girlfriends. While I packed up my stuff in a moving truck, my brother, with his shotgun resting in plain sight on the front seat of his car, threatened Peter to back off.

I felt guilty for leaving because I felt sorry for Peter. He was a hurting man who was deeply insecure and needed someone to love him. Can you believe it? As volatile and sick as our relationship was, I was scared Peter would eventually kill himself. I had known enough suicide victims to understand the reality.

———•———

I moved into the apartment I had rented earlier and started getting closer to one of my friends, Allen, a trick I had actually met in 1992 on a call. We kept in touch over the years; he knew all about Peter and was always encouraging me to get away. A third generation Japanese American man, Allen owned an auto body shop where famous people like Joe Jackson, B.B. King, and entertainers Siegfried & Roy had their cars serviced. Allen was a kind, gentle man who quickly fell in love with me, and I with him. He took me to Hawaii in May 1998, where I stayed blasted with cocaine the entire time. We got engaged on the eighteenth of that month, after Allen begged me to quit the business. "Work for me instead. I'll teach you what I do," he said.

That day I called the escort agency and told them I was done. They informed me I owed them $65,000 in fines, charging me $1,500 a night for calls I couldn't take because I had called in sick, most of them when I was sick from radiation and chemo and could barely stand up, let alone entertain clients. Escort agencies are another form of pimping, another form of sex traffickers. They use you to gain as much money as they can, particularly through these insane fines. I never went on another call from an agency, and I never paid any fines since they were unjustified.

While I was engaged to Allen, I was addicted to cocaine. As high as I was, which was most of the time, I thrived in his shop. Though he had hired me as an office manager, I did a lot more than that. I learned to work on the cars. I sanded them, prepped them for priming, and primed them. It was hard work. And I enjoyed every minute of it.

Allen was also my friend and a fun partner. We worked hard and played just as hard. After a long day, he'd suggest, "Let's go take the kids to Disneyland." And off we would go, taking his little boys on a trek to California to play in the place that made all our dreams come true. Except I would be sneaking bumps between rides and quick cigarettes to get rid of the jitters from the coke.

Toward the end of 1998, we had an opportunity to establish a franchise from Japan in Las Vegas. We had met with Japanese investors who financed five thousand "super shine shops" scattered all across Japan. Catering to luxury cars, these shops offered basic car repair in a short amount of time. Among other things, you could get your dents removed and paint retouched within a few hours. The business thrived in Japan, and these investors gave us a million dollars to start a flagship shop in Las Vegas.

On New Year's Day 1999, Allen helped me quit cocaine cold turkey. We knew that I had to sober up to make our relationship as well as the business work. We had no intention of blowing through the money; we wanted it to be successful. We built an amazing shop with top-of-the-line equipment and, at our height, had eleven employees and were given another million dollars from our investors. We lived the high life, leasing (with an option to buy) a four-thousand-plus-square-foot home on the golf course at Red Rock Country Club. I called this place my "castle." It was beautiful, and I loved it!

I felt on top of the world. Being successful without the need to sell my body increased my confidence. It was like a drug. But the pressure of needing to stay on top in the corporate world was overwhelming. And it was beginning to take a serious toll. We needed high-end accounts to keep up our profit margins, which wasn't an easy task. Eventually I resorted to using my feminine wiles to take advantage of executives and ultimately close deals. I flirted. I propositioned. There's no other way to say it—I used sex to keep the business successful. I wasn't an escort; I was a corporate call girl. I'm not proud of what I did, but at the time I felt I had to work it, to use my prostitution experience, something I was good at, for the good of the company as well as for Allen. He never knew.

Around the same time, the stressors of working long and trying hours started to take a toll on my physical health. I started having intense back problems from being on my feet all day in the storefront and automotive shop we were running. I was introduced to OxyContin by an associate at my corporate job, and the first pill I took not only completely took my back pain away, it also got me extremely high. Instead of feeling stressed and overwhelmed at the pace of business, I felt euphoric. Pretty soon I was doing two pills a day, five pills a day, then seven pills a day, etc. I shopped doctors constantly to keep up my eventual 350mg a day habit. It didn't take long for the euphoria to turn into panic. Truth was, I couldn't keep up the pace of corporate life. And I had a sneaking suspicion that something fishy was happening behind the scenes of our shop. I did the only thing I knew how to do. Hide the stress. Hide the worry. I popped more pills.

A drug addiction is very expensive. I was secretly withdrawing money from our personal savings account to pay for the stuff. Knowing I had to replace the cash so Allen wouldn't be the wiser, I resorted to another familiar solution. I started turning tricks, trafficking myself for drugs. I would walk the carpet of high-class casinos, make money upstairs, and return to the casino floor, a purse full of the replacement cash. But I was greedy. I wanted more. Strung out every time, I didn't go straight home after turning a trick. I'd hit the video poker machines, hoping to double my money so I could finally finish off replacing the money I took. But more often than not, I would lose everything. It was a vicious cycle.

Allen quickly caught on to my addiction and to my reentry into prostitution. "What are you doing?" he yelled with a mixture of concern and anger. I admitted my problem. "I'm addicted to pills, Allen. I can't get off them," I cried. Instead of leaving me to waste away in a sea of drugs, my fiancé got me help. He took me to a doctor who started to wean me off the evil painkillers.

In 2002, three years after we started, our company tanked. An executive from a company in New York had come to analyze the company for future investments, as we intended to expand the business. He ended up stealing our formula for an ultraviolet light and selling it to a global corporation. Allen and I had worked so hard and so fast. We were still waiting for the international patents to come through, so there was nothing we could legally do to stop it. That negligence forced us out of business. Life came crashing down. Not only did we lose our business, we lost our savings and almost everything else as well. We had just enough to open a small auto body shop in order to survive.

I started doing coke again on January 1, 2003, when I learned that we were losing our home on the golf course. I couldn't bear the thought of seeing everything we had worked so hard for ripped away from us. I wanted to disappear into a bottomless pit. I had failed *yet again*. Condemnation beat me down and told me it was my fault, that if I had been a better promoter, manager, etc., this wouldn't have happened. I didn't know what to do. That day I knew the only way to feel better was to go back to the familiar. I started getting the coke on my own, getting high when Allen wasn't around or on business trips out of state.

I'm ashamed at how much money I spent on drugs, as well as what I did to get them. I was out of control. I was doing massive amounts of cocaine and suffering from constant nosebleeds and severe pain, which I would alleviate by popping tons of Sudafed and Motrin. But then my addiction went down an even darker road. Snorting cocaine was no longer enough to get me high. I learned how to cook the refined cocaine with baking soda and water until it formed a hard white rock in a heated pan. I then put it in my glass pipe and took a lighter to it and smoked it. The very thing my first pimp was selling on the street—the one thing that I was so against—became my new friend and confidant. I was so addicted that when I ran out of crack cocaine, I would crawl on the floor on my knees in my beautiful home on the golf course, looking for any rocks I might have dropped by accident while I was getting high. I had seriously reached an all-time low. Up for days on end, sometimes even a week straight, I was smoking coke to try to make the reality of my life's failures disappear into oblivion. I also started smoking about two to three packs of cigarettes a day. Something had to give. There was no way my body could handle how I was slowly destroying it.

While I was pill-free for only a few months, I continued to stay high on coke, pretending that everything was going to be okay, but it wasn't. I was vexed by a spirit of failure and couldn't get over the guilt of the bad choices I had made. On August 2, 2003, I took a big hit of cocaine and walked into the office of our body shop. We had just finished prepping for a $12,000 paint job on, ironically, a pimp's Cadillac Escalade. The minute I inhaled, I felt dizzy. Suddenly I couldn't breathe, the pain in my chest was so intense, and I fell on the floor next to my office chair. Unable to get up, I called out for help. A few seconds later I blacked out.

While I was unconscious, I saw a vision of my funeral. The scene was dark with a bright light spotlighting a coffin. As I walked toward the pine box, I saw me inside. Then I saw my family come up to the coffin, one by one, crying and shaking their heads. "What a waste," someone said. "She was an addicted prostitute. We never knew. What happened to our little girl?" Fear enveloped me as I regained consciousness, staring into the kind eyes of a female paramedic with kinky red hair.

"What seems to be the problem?" she asked.

"I've been doing cocaine," I blurted out, feeling a stabbing pain from every single heartbeat that thumped wildly in my chest. Tears rolled down my eyes as I prayed, "Jesus, help me, please, give me another chance! Please forgive me for all that I have done. I don't want to die. I promise if You save me I will quit everything! I will help others! Please don't let me die like this! Please, Jesus." I then begged the woman not to leave me as she stuck an IV in my arm. I gripped her hand so tightly, I am sure that my nails tore into her flesh.

I was rushed to the hospital, sirens blaring, blue and red lights flashing, learning later I had had a heart attack. A doctor told me I had so many drugs in my blood system that I should have been dead. "There is no medical reason you should be here right now. You're one lucky lady," he said. "God must be with you."

I knew then that God had heard my prayer as I was lying on the office floor, gasping for breath. A sense of divine peace came over me in the hospital room that day. Tears of joy soaked my pillow wet as I thanked God over and over and prayed to

Him to help me heal and get better. I knew at that point in time I would never again touch drugs or prostitute myself for money. I didn't want it, crave it, or thirst for it. I was instantly delivered from my addictions to cocaine, smoking, and painkillers.

While I knew that was nothing short of a miracle, my relational life was still a disaster. I was severely broken in my heart, and I knew it was going to take more than a rock-bottom moment to get me well.

The good and glorious news was that I knew I was *done*! No more going back. No more staying up all night for days on end getting high. No more desperate thoughts of running away from myself and hiding from the cruel world. No more night-mares of wearing a mask, pretending everything had turned out perfectly. I finally took the mask of pretention off. Fallen died that night. The masquerade was over, and this girl was done dancing to frenzied music stringed with despair and remorse. My whole life in the sex industry had been a façade. I knew that my old life was now over, and a new one was beginning! And the beauty of everything was this: I had to realize that my life was a disaster so I could awaken to the glorious change God was about to do. Only after catastrophic disaster can we be beauti-fully resurrected.

I was on my way to a beautiful place of redemption and promise. Hello, sweet Jesus, here I come.

CHAPTER 9

LEARNING TO FLY

"I'll spread my wings and I'll learn how to fly
I'll do what it takes till I touch the sky."
—Kelly Clarkson, "Breakaway"

My physical recovery after the hospital lasted a few weeks. Allen nursed me back to health, making sure I ate healthy foods and drank enough water. Sleep was hard to come by. I thank God for Allen, because he was really there for me during this diffi-cult transition in my life. Though my doctor had prescribed sleeping pills so I could get adequate rest, I refused to take them. I was scared. I didn't want to fuel another addiction and was completely determined to stay off any narcotics.

The TV became my faithful bedside companion as I woke up at odd hours during the night after tossing and turning. It was hard to sleep because of all the remorse, guilt, and shame I felt from my overdose and from my past. One particular night, unable to get complete rest as usual, I tuned into infomercials of blenders and exercise equipment before settling the channel on a loud and bold woman named Joyce Meyer. Her words instantly reeled me in. I had never before heard anyone describe God the way she did. She spoke of how God was a Healer, a Vindicator, a Giver of grace. And not just for special people who did the right things all of the time but for everyone, for people even like me, a woman most would label with a scarlet letter for selling her body. Was God really like how she described Him? I had to find out! I don't know if I refused to believe it at the time because it sounded too good to be true.

So I leaned in. Kept watching. You do that when you're hungry and thirsty for something you've sampled that fills you. I wanted more. I was focused on learning whatever I could. That night, something deeper happened. There was a defining moment when Joyce said, "God loves you, no matter what you have done, where you have been. He loves you right where you are." At those words, my heart melted.

Seriously? God loves me? After all I've done?

For the first time in my life, I heard God's voice speaking directly into my heart. "Yes, Annie. I love you. And there is *nothing* that will separate you from My love" (Romans 8:38–39). I got it. I finally got it! As tears welled up in my eyes, I got down on my knees before the TV and humbled myself with repentance. I prayed, "God, if this is true, show me—I want this love to change me. I know I'm messed up, and I've done some really bad things, but I can't do this without You. I dedicate my entire life to You, Jesus, and I need Your help."

God loves me. Those words struck a chord in my songless heart that night and started a new melody of grace. Oh beautiful grace! He gave me a reason to sing a new song, praising God for all that He had done. I finally had the nerve, the courage, the desire to believe everything good He had for me. In that moment, my faith walk toward God became so much deeper than just the desperation of the overdose, the pain, or my bad choices. I dedicated my entire life to Jesus. I surrendered the pain. I surrendered the disappointments. I surrendered the shame. I surrendered the guilt. Psalm 40:3 says, "May many see what God has done, so that they might swear allegiance to him and trust in the LORD" (NET). I saw this love. I saw what He had done. I welcomed this Truth, and it had nothing to do with a man, materialism, drugs, money, or fantasies. That day I found the truth in who God was—my faithful, merciful, loving, heavenly Father.

Even through a television screen, filmed in another part of the country, Joyce's words breathed such sweet life into me. She made God real to me for the first time in my life. She understood my pain and shame, as she had endured years of sexual abuse at the hands of her own father. The hope in God she offered was a beacon of light in the dark and cold cave of my soul. Pretty soon I started getting up in the wee hours of the morning automatically, just before her show came on. She became my daily mentor and my spiritual mom. She was a shining example of an overcomer making it through the darkness to the other side. God used her to ignite a renewed hope in my life, something that I had lost so long ago. I knew if she could make it, somehow I could too.

Allen bought me my first fancy Amplified Bible. While he didn't believe in God yet, he was completely blown away by my transformation. He could see changes in me from my new mannerisms, how I took care of myself, and my whole happy and hopeful attitude. I was happy for the first time in my life!

And instead of reaching out for pills or cocaine, for material things to fix me and relationships to comfort me; I relied instead on Jesus' love for me. His love did something to me that Satan's counterfeit love never could. It gave me security so that I could trust God with my pain. I didn't have to fear like I did in my past. When I was in the sex industry, I often feared that I would never have the love that I longed for. So I filled myself with material things and fake relationships to try to quiet those fears deep in my heart that I was unlovable. This fear and anxiety became such a burden to me as I continued to search and search for meaning, for answers. I was relieved to know that I no longer had to carry every burden that I had taken upon myself. I held on to the truth of Matthew 11:28 day and night when I felt the pain of emotional healing was more than I could bear: "Come to me, all you who are weary and burdened, and I will give you rest."

I also started eating better, trading a diet lacking in nutrition for fresh juices and vegan meals. I devoured the entire Bible—I could not get enough of it. The Bible's words were full of life, healing to my body and spirit. I read a lot of spiritually uplifting books by Joyce Meyer, such as *Battlefield of the Mind* and *Beauty for Ashes*, as well as *The Purpose Driven Life* by Rick Warren and *The Bait of Satan* by John Bevere and *Kissed the Girls and Made Them Cry* by his wife, Lisa Bevere. Lisa was also a friend/mentor to me. She kept in contact with me and lovingly guided me into understanding my new life as a newbie Christian seeking God's heart. Through studying Scripture and reading these and other books, I began to grow in my faith walk. I even connected with a few strong Christian women who mentored me, one in Minnesota long distance (Jayne) and one locally in

Vegas (Pastor Denise). They helped walk me through the baby stages of my new adventure with faith.

God's Word was my lifeline. I was desperate, thirsty, and hungry for true change, and I knew what I was looking for was no longer unavailable, it was living deep within me (Jesus) and in the pages of my Bible. The truth was that my thought patterns were so messed up from the horrific lifestyle I had lived. (I didn't realize it at the time, but I later discovered that I had post-traumatic stress disorder.) I knew I needed a radical change inside my mind and heart. I knew that if I could find some answers for my depravity and the crazy life I lived, God would be faithful to continue to reveal more truth to me. Truth to refute the lies Satan had me tricked into believing for so long! That I was unlovable, that no one would ever forgive me, that my past would always be my enemy, that I would forever be labeled a "whore."

But in the Bible, I read the many beautiful yet some-times tragic stories of people who were a lot like me—broken, depressed, doubtful, fearful, prideful, messed up. These stories were like treasures of light to my darkened soul! And I was so thirsty for them. Cisterns of free-flowing waters channeled themselves to my dry and cracked heart.

Stories about Rahab, a harlot who was rescued by the Israelites; Tamar and Judah, a trick and a desperate prostitute; Abram, who almost sold his wife, Sarai, to a pharaoh to gain riches; Hosea, the husband whom God told to marry the harlot Gomer; the woman at the well with five ex-husbands and a live-in lover; the woman caught in adultery to whom Jesus gave mercy instead of judgment; a sinful woman who anointed Jesus' feet with perfume from an alabaster box; and even more. These stories and more nursed and healed my battered and bruised body and soul.

There was nothing else that could explain this amazing epiphany, this incredible, powerful, and wonderful awakening in my life. I was falling in love with Jesus, and I couldn't get enough of Him. Like a lover, He chased me, wooed me, and spoke life into me. I craved His presence wherever I went. When I went to bed every night, I would fall asleep reading my Bible, hugging it tightly to my chest. When I woke up in the morning, I would immediately put on worship music and read my Bible again. I was so thankful I was alive and breathing to live another day. This was a precious gift—this gift of my second chance. I knew I didn't deserve it—but yet Jesus' mercy and grace allowed me to have it. Every morning I would ask Jesus what He wanted me to do that day for Him, eager to serve and help others. I was so full of joy, so full of peace, so full of His love. I was extremely hopeful. Hopeful He would continue to change me inside where I needed it the most. Hopeful of the special plans He had for me. Hopeful I could share His love with others and be used to change their lives.

I remember I was pursuing God with all my heart and my soul—nothing could satisfy this deep desire but Him. I was a God chaser. And I continually asked for *more* because my hunger to change my perspective and heal was so intense. That "more" God provided. I was on my God journey in Orlando, Florida, in 2004 at a Joyce Meyer conference when Joyce gave an altar call to receive the Holy Spirit. I didn't completely understand everything that meant at the time, but I knew I had to have the Holy Spirit if I was to continue to grow in my walk with Jesus. The Holy Spirit gives us power and the ability to do the things that God has called us to do. I had read Acts 1:8, which says, "But you will receive power when the Holy Spirit comes on you; and you will be my witnesses in Jerusalem, and in all Judea and Samaria, and to the ends of the earth."

I had also learned from Romans 8:11 that it was the Holy Spirit's life-giving power that raised Jesus from the dead, and I wanted more. "The Spirit of God, who raised Jesus from the dead, lives in you. And just as God raised Christ Jesus from the dead, he will give life to your mortal bodies by this same Spirit living within you" (NLT).

When I do things, I am the type of person who doesn't settle for halfway; I'm all in 100 percent of whatever it is. That's what made me a successful escort—I was all in. How much more could God use this good attitude, now that I was on the other side? Mama Joyce said the prayer, and I prayed to receive the Holy Spirit, and specifically I wanted the gift of speaking in tongues that I had read about in Acts 2:4 and 10:46. I waited, and nothing happened. I opened my eyes to peek to see what the other ten thousand-plus women were doing, because at this point, more than half had stood up to receive the Holy Spirit. At first I was disappointed that I didn't get the gift of tongues on that trip, but at the same time I felt a newness and power I had never experienced before, so I knew that God had faithfully filled me with more of His Spirit and had done a work in me. A little bit tearful, I prayed to God, telling Him that I didn't understand why I didn't get the manifestation of tongues, but that if it wasn't His will for me, it was okay, just as long as He was living in me and was empowering me in all my endeavors. It's funny what happens when you surrender your will, because that was the very moment I was filled! I felt God's Spirit prompt me to open my mouth and speak, and all of a sudden I started speaking in tongues. Many of you reading this might not understand what this is, so do your own personal research on it. All I can tell you is that it was glorious! I was even more empowered to continue on with God.

This brought me to a whole new level of miracles and breakthroughs. People started to make fun of me and laugh at how radical I had become. I got ridiculed and called a lot of names like "Jesus freak" and "religious nut," but I didn't care. Honestly, I was too happy to care. Let them laugh! Let them make fun of me because I had been changed. *Nothing* else mattered to me in my life but my new walk with God. It was so precious to me, I shuddered at the very thought of ever losing it. When you find something that valuable, you will do whatever it takes to keep it . . . you *never* let it go.

Matthew 13:44 says, "The kingdom of heaven is like a treasure hidden in the field, which a man found and hid again; and from joy over it he goes and sells all that he has and buys that field" (NASB). I was living in the kingdom of heaven, and I felt like I was finally *home*.

At first I thought I was the one who chose God, but the more I read the Bible, the more I understood that He actually chose *me*. One passage that really spoke to me during this time was Jeremiah 1:5: "Before I formed you in the womb I knew [and] approved of you [as My chosen instrument], and before you were born I separated and set you apart, consecrating you; [and] I appointed you as a prophet to the nations" (AMP). So that entire time I was living a crazy lifestyle of sex, drugs, and rock and roll? Yep. God knew I was going to do it, yet He still chose *me*!

God desired and pursued me like a respectable gentleman. He never pushed Himself on me. He was ever so gentle. Love isn't pushy, fretful, boastful, or envious. Above all, it is patient, kind, and long-suffering (1 Corinthians 13:4–7). He picked me up and set me apart, just for His special use. And even though I didn't know what that special use was yet, and I would often question Him, I knew I could trust Him. He knew my thoughts, just like it says in Psalm 139:2. He numbered the hairs on my head (Luke 12:7); not counted them, *individually* numbered them! He collected my tears if I was having a bad day (Psalm 56:8). He ordained me when I thought I was a lost cause. He sanctified me when I didn't think I was good enough to help others. He made me know that I was special. I wasn't meant to walk with the crowd any longer. And I was so relieved that I did not have to be like everyone else! Becoming an individual in Christ gave my life a whole new meaning. There is a reason why we all have different fingerprints—because He has a unique plan for each and every one of us! God planned my life for a designated purpose because He knew the good I would do with it. It felt so good to be trusted again. When you are trusted, *you feel loved.*

God is the only One who could speak a word of life to my heart from the terrible tragedies I experienced. He is the only One who could open a door to my future and make me believe that I could walk through that door as a triumphant champion. Jeremiah 29:11 was another scripture I clung to, because I just *knew* deep down inside that God had an amazing plan for me: "For I know the thoughts and plans that I have for you, says the Lord, thoughts and plans for welfare and peace and not for evil, to give you hope in your final outcome" (AMP).

As I devoured the Bible, one of the first things I learned was about my identity in Christ. In my past, I had let the media and culture define who I was. How thin I was supposed to be, how pretty I was to look, what kind of car I should drive, where I needed to live, and how much money was needed in my bank account. The truth was that media and culture did nothing but lie to me. None of those things made me happier, smarter, or prettier. I was so tired of the peer pressure to be perfect, of trying to make everyone like me and accept me for what they saw on the outside. So I took a stand. I no longer wanted to live with a mask to please others. In my old life, I was always worried about what people thought about me and allowed that worry to control me like a god. So I would give whatever I had financially, physically, emotionally, and spiritually to others in hopes they would give me back what I needed. I thought I needed them to love me. But the truth is, they never really did. They loved what I gave them, but did not love me as a person. After I started my new life, I decided that if God could accept me for who I was without any strings attached, then people who truly loved me would accept me too. And even if they didn't, so be it. It was their loss!

I knew that God had an amazing plan for me no matter who was rejecting me. When others reject you because they aren't getting their way, you must realize they are only manipulating you for what they can get from you. Who wants a friend like that? Anyone who needs to control you is really not your friend! The conviction hit me hard—that I couldn't live this way any longer because it nearly destroyed me. The more I learned about how God had created me to be a unique, strong, gifted woman for the good work He had assigned me to do on this earth, the more I was determined to be obedient to Him. Honestly, this was a fantastic discovery to know that I could truly be me and that God still loved me, and I did not have to feel guilty about not pleasing others.

A new level of freedom rose up in me. I knew I was called by Him. Set apart. "But you are a chosen race, a royal priesthood, a holy nation, a people for his own possession, that you may proclaim the excellencies of him who called you out of darkness into his marvelous light" (1 Peter 2:9 ESV). I was in darkness, chosen, and to top it off, I was part of Jesus' family, and if He was royalty, that made me as His heir royalty too. Wow! Maybe the Disney fantasy was at least on the right track . . . castles, carriages, princes, and princesses? Hey, a girl can dream, right?

I also learned that the devil had a wicked and evil plan for my life. John 10:10 says that the devil comes *only* to steal, kill, and destroy. The enemy knew if I had an identity crisis, he could get me to believe that I needed to change and conform to people and the world's culture. And that's how he manipulates us. He uses things and people to tempt us to believe that these "things" are going to make us happy if we just continue to accumulate more. But the more we get, the emptier we all become.

Adam and Eve learned the same thing in the garden of Eden. Satan convinces us that if we will bite the fruit that God has clearly told us to stay away from, we will become like mini-gods, in control of our destinies. Sure, sin is always fun in the beginning—and I am not going to lie, I enjoyed it very much for a season. But the guilt, shame, regret, and repercussions that come with it weren't worth it! Rebellion always leads to ruin. If we follow the customs and practices of this world, we eventually end up being puppet-mastered by Satan's lures of materialism and man-worship. He almost had me! The puppet I lived as for years was named Fallen. He made Fallen believe she could live with the mask of pretense, lies, and the spirit of Jezebel's greed for more. But the devil messed up big-time . . . he forgot that I am an heir to the throne. His plans were null and void as soon as Jesus died on that cross. Satan forgot that my own dying to self would expose all his wicked lies! God uses tragedies and failures like mine for His purpose (Romans 8:28). God had a greater plan no matter what crazy things I had done. And it was to use the pain that almost destroyed me from my past for the good of others.

Learning all of these incredible revelations was better than any high I had ever experienced. When the darkness of lies was swept away and Truth was revealed, I could finally see the world in a whole new light. I was like Dorothy from *The Wizard of Oz* walking out of her house and her black-and-white world into a land of Technicolor rainbow beauty for the very first time.

Allen and I broke up in February 2005. We loved each other, but we were committed to different things. While I was so thankful for the relationships I had with him and his family, and all the truly wonderful things he taught me and showed me, I knew that staying with him could no longer be because we weren't married. I felt the conviction of the Holy Spirit that I needed to end our relationship. (Both of Allen's boys, Jaden and Justin, whom I love dearly and was blessed to raise with Allen for eight years, saw the change in me and both professed their belief in Jesus. Eventually Allen followed suit and got saved a year later.) To this day, we are all still good friends, and he and his family are very proud of me.

I felt God calling me to help other women in the sex-trafficking industry, but I wasn't sure how or in what way.

I continued to seek God for guidance and direction. I was so determined at this point to make a lasting change that I refused to let anything stop me. I became very aggressive and jealous for my alone time with God. I couldn't get enough time with Him, and I only wanted more! I sincerely wanted God to be my closest friend, to touch Him, know Him, feel Him, and see Him. As strange as this may sound, ever since my conversion, I prayed to see the face of Jesus. I was falling in love, and I wondered what He looked like. I wanted to see His eyes, to look into them to see the truth, to see Him for who He really is: God. Did He really forgive all of my sins? Did He know how much I loved Him? What was His exact plan for me? Could He really keep loving me, even though I continued to make mistakes as a new Christian? Trust me, I was not perfect in the least as I was learning. I still struggled in so many things, I messed up more times than I could count!

And then God answered my prayer. I had a dream one night that I was sitting at a bus stop in New York City. A man with long brown hair dressed in a flowing robe started walking toward me. I was immediately supernaturally drawn to Him and couldn't keep my eyes off of Him. Something in me just *knew* it was Jesus. He was strikingly beautiful, with strong facial features, chiseled in defining angles. His eyes, one crystal blue, the other emerald green, were radiant with light. A foot or two of distance between us, we stood facing each other for some time, His arms reaching out toward me. In this moment, I couldn't help but feel the most intense embodiment of love and peace. I didn't want the dream to end. Finally, He drew closer, inches away from my face. As Jesus looked at me with the most deep, intense, loving stare, He finally spoke, not with His mouth, but with eyes that reached deep into my soul.

Annie, I see you. And I have witnessed everything terrible you have been through. I am the God who sees. I am the God who cares. It wasn't right what was done to you. But that doesn't matter now, for I am here. You're not alone, and you never will be as long you believe that I am here with you. I will always be with you. I've always been here, from the moment you were born until now. Do you know why? Because I've loved you from the beginning of time.

You're My precious daughter. You are My royal heritage. I have so many plans for you, daughter! You are healed from your broken heart—I have made you whole. The tragedies you have been through in your life will be used as a bridge to heal others. You don't have to worry about the rest of your life and what will happen because I am the One who planned your life and birth. Trust in Me in all things. I will be your sustenance and life now.

Everything bad you've ever experienced is going to work out in your favor. I have an incredible purpose for you that no one else can fulfill. I want you to go down to the Las Vegas Strip and tell the women who are enslaved that I love them. Tell them how healing My love is for their broken hearts. Show them how it has made you change for the better. Tell them how much you've

been healed from your pain and that you are
now whole. Tell them they can also have or can,
too, have what you have if they could give all
their burdens to Me.

In this vision, Jesus looked at me with such tenderness and compassion. He saw everything I had ever done, good and bad, and everything that had once created fear and pain in me. I was not embarrassed or ashamed when I stood in front of Him. I simply felt incredibly loved and at peace. He really did heal me. He truly made me whole in that moment. I knew it, I felt it. But more than that, He was calling me to a greater purpose, something I didn't have to run from anymore. I was home. Home not just to feel good, but home to make a difference in the lives of others. It's an indescribable feeling I will never be able to adequately share in words. Tears flow from my eyes as I write this story . . .

When I woke up, I didn't remember the dream right away. Later that afternoon, as I was vacuuming my bedroom, I remembered seeing Jesus in my dream. I immediately fell to my knees, bringing to mind His words. I cried tears of joy and lay there in awe, soaking in His warm presence. That day the unique calling I felt to help women was confirmed. Though I instinctively knew it would happen someday, I wasn't naive. I knew I still had some inner work to do.

While Christ instantaneously delivered me from my addiction to drugs, He continually worked in me to make me emotionally and mentally sound. Second Corinthians 3:16–18 says:

Whenever, though, they turn to face God as
Moses did, God removes the veil and there they

are—face-to-face! They suddenly recognize that God is a living, personal presence, not a piece of chiseled stone. And when God is personally present, a living Spirit, that old, constricting legislation is recognized as obsolete. We're free of it! All of us! Nothing between us and God, our faces shining with the brightness of his face. And so we are transfigured much like the Messiah, our lives gradually becoming brighter and more beautiful as God enters our lives and we become like him (MSG).

The New American Standard Bible says that we are changed from "glory to glory." I had so much deep-rooted pain, rejection, and heartbreak that had been with me ever since I was a little girl. God showed me the places that needed to be healed little by little over time. If He had revealed everything to me at once, it would have been a disaster, and I might have quit. God knew this. It was a slow process, complete with a lot of studying, worshiping, praying, wrestling with God, surrendering, and the shedding of many painful tears.

Though I was not chained anymore to the shame of my past, I still grieved over dark secrets I had kept. I had a total of seven abortions and three miscarriages over the years that had built in me a flood of overwhelming shame, guilt, and regret to add to the layers that were already present. Oh, how the thoughts of what I had done in my past haunted me and screamed obscenities at me late into the night. The guilt would grab my heart and the shame would overwhelm me, flooding me with condemning reminders of what a "bad girl" I was, how incredibly selfish I was, what a terrible and underserving mother I was. Every time I saw a baby with a mother laughing and cooing, the knife of sharp guilt would pierce my gut, reminding me that I was a murderer of my children. And it was absolutely, utterly true that I was.

I had lied my way through most of my life in the sex industry. Lied to every trick, lied to my parents, lied to my family, lied about my abortions. I pretended I was okay when I was not—that I enjoyed what I did for a living when in reality I hated being touched and treated like an object to men. Layers of these lies covering up my life consumed me and tormented me, and it was too heavy for me to bear. I hated myself.

In my past, I couldn't handle loving another human being because I thought I was unlovable myself. I reasoned bringing a child into my personal hell of the sex industry and the pimp world was selfish. And I was a coward. Too fearful to go through with the pregnancies. Too afraid that my child would continue the lineage of pimps and hoes. Too fearful my pimp would stalk me and come after me because of the child connection. To add to the excuses, my abortion doctor continually enforced his beliefs on me, that the fetus isn't a human until five months or more and not to worry about getting rid of something that was not technically alive. I now know those things are not true because I have since learned about the stages of a baby's development. Despite all those justifications, I still had this feeling and knowing in my spirit that what I did was absolutely wrong.

Before I quit drugs and escorting, I would often get high to escape those damning and condemning feelings of helplessness, shame, and regret. What do you do when you can't let go of the terrible things you have done? When you are so brokenhearted you cannot forgive yourself? We must not run but face this pain. You must decide no matter how terrible you feel, to forgive yourself, trusting that God has forgiven you too.

How do we forgive ourselves? God saw my broken heart, and He heard my prayers of repentance for what I had done. Psalm 34:18 says, "The LORD is close to the brokenhearted; he rescues those whose spirits are crushed" (NLT). And while He knew the reasons I had ended my pregnancies weren't His plan, He knew I was very sorry, and that I needed to receive His grace and mercy to set me free. It was a gift He was trying to give me, but I hadn't opened up my hand to receive it. You see, there is *no* condemnation in Christ Jesus when we are set free from our sin (Romans 8:1)!

But the devil had been condemning me, taking advantage of my guilt and banking that I would keep my closet door shut, never allowing the skeletons to tell another soul about my deep, dark secrets. But the closet door was about to finally pop open.

I will never forget on Mother's Day of 2005, I was crying in my rented room, and God and I had a conversation. I prayed and told God how sorry I was for what I had done. Remember what it says in the last part of Psalm 34:18: "He rescues those whose spirits are crushed"? God came down to rescue me to give me a love touch. And I opened my hand to receive His mercy gift. I suddenly felt His presence fall over me so deeply, so tangibly in the room. Peace entered me, and I heard a voice say to me, "Annie, I forgave you for this the first time you asked Me—when you had every single one of them. I have your children. They are safe with Me. Don't worry anymore. If I have forgiven you, I want you to follow My lead and learn to let go and forgive yourself. By the way, I'm not mad at you . . . I still love you." He loved me *still*. After all that I had done to destroy His creation. Wow. How good is our God? Tears and sobbing ensued, and then a gentle peace overcame my soul.

That Mother's Day I was released from my prison of self-blame, shame, guilt, condemnation, and regret. Understanding the love God had for me made it easier to forgive myself for the sin of ending those particular pregnancies, as well as the painful miscarriages lost. If Jesus could forgive me, surely I could forgive myself. I could not let my feelings rule my life anymore and destroy the awesome things God had for me. I decided to forgive myself, and though it felt awkward at first, as each day passed I felt more and more grace and mercy and love fall upon me from Jesus. Forgiving myself became a precious treasure that opened up a whole new level of freedom. It is truly a great revelation, knowing that God loves you and forgives you—no matter what crazy and terrible things you have done. And even when you've run to incredibly dark places in hopes of running from the pain, He still waits for you, welcoming you with open arms of mercy and grace when you're ready.

CHAPTER 10

ARMS WIDE OPEN

*"I have held many things in my hands, and I have lost
them all; but whatever I have placed in God's hands, that
I still possess."*
—Martin Luther

Love never keeps treasures for itself. Love never holds forgiveness over someone's head as a debt. Love gives. Love reaches. Love does. And it lays its very life down for another.

Jesus gave the gift of His life (John 3:16) because He loved us first. He died to forgive us. All of us have made a mess of things in our own lives (I know I have!), and we desperately need His loving arms to comfort us and wrap around us. To teach us that if we trust in Him and His goodness, He will make all things new when everything seems destroyed and lost.

I don't know what your situation is. You may be a sex worker or know someone who is. Maybe you are in an abusive relationship. Maybe you prostitute yourself not for money but for love, for affection, for approval. Maybe you've been sexually abused or addicted to drugs or alcohol. Maybe you suffer from the psychological repercussions of a traumatic or tragic situation. Or maybe you simply feel spiritually lost, believing that God doesn't see you, care about you, or even love you.

I want to breathe hope into you the same way I was ministered to when I left the game. Let me tell you something— *you matter!* What you have been through is very important to God! He sees you. You are not alone. Because I have been saved, healed, and restored, I am not the woman I was. As a matter of fact, what the devil tried to use to destroy my life, God flipped around and is using to empower me to help others. I love what Genesis 50:20 tells us: "You intended to harm me, but God intended it for good to accomplish what is now being done, the saving of many lives." Even though people have used me, sold me, and thrown me away, I have chosen to forgive them, and God has miraculously changed me for the better so I can show others that what they have been through was never meant to be discarded like a piece of trash. Their experiences are treasures that can be used to help others—to show that God is a good God and His love will lead us out of slavery and into freedom, no matter what terrible things have taken place. No bad thing I have done can ever haunt me again. My guilt and shame have been removed!

As my healing continued, I knew I also needed to extend forgiveness to those who had harmed me. My father and I have reconciled our rocky relationship. I love my dad, and I know he loves me. We are closer than we've ever been. And I have even forgiven my pimp! Would you believe I actually pray for him every day, hopeful he will one day believe in Jesus and turn his life around? I want Julian to know that he, too, can be redeemed and that God really loves him, even while he is living a life without God. In his mistakes, in his pain, in his seeking out happiness and never finding it. That kind of compassion can come only from the all-transforming work of the love of Jesus.

Now, I'm not saying that the abuse Julian inflicted on me was at all okay. Forgiveness doesn't minimize the offense; it's more about you than the person who has done you wrong. Forgiving Julian was one of the bridges I had to cross on my way to true freedom. Not forgiving him wasn't going to make him pay for his actions; it just made me more miserable. And who in their right mind wants to be miserable?

A few months after I had been diagnosed with cancer, I was at a club with some friends. After a night of partying, I left the hotspot as the sun made its way up over the horizon. As I headed to my car, I saw Julian nearby. While my first instinct was to run, instead I froze. Make no mistake, I was petrified, but something about him seemed different, calm.

Julian looked at me, sheepish almost, with tears in his eyes, and said words I never thought in a million years that I would hear. "Fallen, I wanted to tell you I'm really sorry for all the times I beat you. You were a good woman, and I never treated you right. Frankly, I didn't know what I had." His apology was heartfelt and sincere. As much as my emotions swirled in my heart, that day I believed he meant it.

It's so easy to get mad at the pimps orchestrating the game and even the johns for paying for sex. But being angry will not win them to Christ. Neither will hate, judgment, revenge, or malice. Some men in this sex business are being used and tricked into it through pornography. Men weren't born to be johns or destined to be pimps. They weren't created with evil and hardened hearts wanting to traffic and use girls. Something, maybe a painful, traumatic, or abusive experience, led up to that perverse desire. I also believe these men harbor an empty place in their hearts with a hunger for love that can only be filled by Christ. They desperately need Jesus just as much as the next person does.

Instead of pointing fingers, we *all* need to look inside ourselves and see the truth of the wrong things we do, even things similar to prostitution. How many of us pursue the American dream with a fierce passion, leaving behind in the dust families who ache for our companionship? The purpose of life is not about accumulating and worshiping material things we think will fill in our empty spots. It's not about living in the best zip code, having the trophy spouse, getting the dream job, or having a hefty bank account. Material prosperity of the American dream is nothing more than a lie. I see it as corporate prostitution. A massive mirage in the desert!

Think about it. If you don't sell your body sexually, you can sell yourself trying to keep up with the Joneses by working long hours, accumulating stress, and never seeing your family so you can continue to live in that huge house and drive that fancy car. You can sell yourself by diluting your mind with idealistic fantasies and theories about how to live a fulfilling life outside of God. This is part of the devil's plan. His desire is for us all to prostitute ourselves in some way, to distract us from our need for God, to sell our bodies, our minds, our souls, and our hearts for what we falsely believe is the dangled golden carrot of the pursuit of happiness. It says in the Bible that anything we put on the altar and worship is an idol (Exodus 20:3–6). How many of us as consumers put ourselves on the altar with our entitlement mentalities and ended up pimping ourselves? Or let the items we worship pimp us?

Are you tired? Are you done fighting? Are you weary of putting your trust in materialism? Success? Fame? Fortune? Others? None of these things will ever make you happy. In fact, they can make your heart sick with emptiness. You will never fill the hole in your heart with the things in this world because they will all be destroyed eventually. Don't believe me? Go look at a junkyard and see what you find. Items that were once treasures are now decomposing and rusting away.

There is a story of the woman at the well in John 4:1–42. She had had five husbands and now had a live-in boyfriend. She came to the well at high noon, probably so no one would see her and ridicule or judge her. She was probably hiding from others. No one knows for sure. She came for water, to quench her thirst, and she had a large pot with her to fill at Jacob's well. Jesus met her there, and even though Jewish men weren't supposed to talk to women like her (she was a Samaritan), Jesus asked her if she would give Him a drink. The crazy thing is that *she* was the one who was thirsty.

> When a Samaritan woman came to draw water, Jesus said to her, "Will you give me a drink?" (His disciples had gone into the town to buy food.)
>
> The Samaritan woman said to him, "You are a Jew and I am a Samaritan woman. How can you ask me for a drink?" (For Jews do not associate with Samaritans.)
>
> Jesus answered her, "If you knew the gift of God and who it is that asks you for a drink, you

*would have asked him and he would have given
you living water."*

*"Sir," the woman said, "you have nothing to
draw with and the well is deep. Where can you
get this living water? Are you greater than our
father Jacob, who gave us the well and drank
from it himself, as did also his sons and his
livestock?"*

*Jesus answered, "Everyone who drinks this
water will be thirsty again, but whoever drinks
the water I give them will never thirst. Indeed, the
water I give them will become in them a spring
of water welling up to eternal life." (vv. 7–14)*

This woman, who was clearly thirsty, spiritually, romantically, relationally . . . tired of life, tired of bad relationships, tired
of searching and never finding happiness . . . finally found the
living water of Jesus to quench her ravaging thirst inside of her
spirit and soul. She had a heart change that day, and as soon
as she found out that Jesus was the prophesied Messiah, she set
down her empty pot and ran to tell others in town that she had
met the Messiah, Jesus.

I can relate to this woman so much. I have been in the very
same place she has, searching but never finding, looking but
never seeing, wanting but never being satisfied.

How about you? Where are you? Are you in the desert
looking for water, but every time you get to it, it disappears like
a mirage, never quenching that deep need you have spiritually?
Many of the aches and desires we feel can be traced to a spiritual
need that we are longing to fulfill but don't know how.

The desire for change must come from the heart, because that is where real change takes place—from a heart that is famished, thirsty, tired, and ready for that change. Proverbs 4:23 says, "Watch over your heart with all diligence, for from it flow the springs of life" (NASB).

Are you thirsty for change? Change must occur in spirit and in truth. If you make changes in your life without paying attention to your heart, the change will only be temporary. It will not take permanent root. You must surrender the desire for more or for something you idolize in your heart. What are you running from? It's high time to stop running in the desert of dryness and *come home.*

> *Is anyone thirsty?*
>   *Come and drink—*
>   *even if you have no money!*
> *Come, take your choice of wine or milk—*
> *it's all free!*
> *Why spend your money on food that does*
>   *not give you strength?*
> *Why pay for food that does you no good?*
> *Listen to me, and you will eat what is good.*
> *You will enjoy the finest food.*
>
> *Come to me with your ears wide open.*
> *Listen, and you will find life.*
> *I will make an everlasting covenant*
>   *with you.*
> *I will give you all the unfailing love*
>   *I promised to David.*

> *See how I used him to display my power*
>   *among the peoples.*
> *I made him a leader among the nations.*
> *You also will command nations you do*
>   *not know,*
> *and peoples unknown to you will come*
>   *running to obey,*
> *because I, the LORD your God,*
> *the Holy One of Israel, have made you glorious.*
> (Isaiah 55:1–5 NLT)

Whatever your life situation, whatever the root of your pain, heartache, guilt, or shame, you can come to the other side. You don't have to live in misery, despair, and emptiness any longer. You can do more than just survive; you can overcome! You can become part of God's kingdom here on earth and start enjoying and living the life you've always wanted. But you can't do this by simply wishing, dreaming, or fantasizing about it. You have to take action. You have to step out in faith and believe that God can love someone like you. Listen, Jesus loved everyone, the prostitutes, the bums, the tax collectors, the liars, thieves, the judgmental people, the religious Pharisees! He does and will love you too.

You have to let go of everything that lies behind you and make a commitment to allow God to change your heart and do the work that is required, even if the transformation process is difficult or it hurts. I know it will be hard, but trust me, it is so worth every tear, every heartache, every lonesome night to choose to do what's right. You can press through the pain because God is on your side.

What have you got to lose? It's time to surrender. Surrender your pride, surrender your fears, and surrender your need for control. Surrender your questions of why you think God has allowed your life to turn out like it has. Surrender the questions you have of how God can change your life; just trust Him that He *will* do it. When you take a step of faith, you are a step closer to experiencing a radical life makeover.

God will meet you right where you are, just like Jesus met the woman at the well. You don't have to get all cleaned up and be perfect before you ask for His help. He desires you just as you are. He isn't judgmental; He is merciful. He isn't prejudiced; He is unconditionally loving. He isn't cruel; He is compassionate. God wants you, dirty baggage and all. He desires an intimate relationship with you like you've never known before.

You can be loved by God, who believes in you and cares for you! You can live out the purpose God specifically designed for you. As I've said before, you must first surrender everything unconditionally to Him. And that means surrendering your *total* will to Him. Many come to God just so He will fix their problems, and there is nothing wrong with that. God will use that to draw us to Him if He needs to. But God doesn't just want to fix our problems, He wants *all* of us. Romans 12:1 says, "And so, dear brothers and sisters, I plead with you to give your bodies to God because of all he has done for you. Let them be a living and holy sacrifice—the kind he will find acceptable. This is truly the way to worship him" (NLT).

And remember, He is a gentleman and won't force this surrender on us; rather, He waits patiently for the moment when we decide that living our life outside of His will has become a dangerous and disastrous mess, and we are finally sick of it!

You might say, "But, Annie, how do I know if I surrender my life to Him that He is going to take care of me and actually help me?" Okay, yeah, I get it—trust me. I surrendered to my pimp and all the crazy mess that came with it . . . and look where that got me! Nothing but heartache! But you have to remember that was *men*, not God. People will always let you down, because everyone is human and makes mistakes. But God is different— He is our Father, our Designer, the One who created us—so if we are broken, it is obvious He is the only One who can fix us! Why wouldn't you go to the designer who made you when you have discovered you are broken? Only a fool wouldn't. When we surrender our lives to Him, He gives us His resurrected life so that He may live in us and through us. Seriously, what could you not gain from fully trusting Him, when you have already lost everything anyway?

The next step after you have surrendered is to live out what you have asked God for. If you asked Him to take over your life, you must decide to give Him complete control. You have to trust Him no matter how you feel. I am not going to lie to you, this won't be a smooth ride. For me, walking out my healing was extremely painful. I wanted to stop more times than I can count. But something in me refused to quit. I had to decide to believe God's promises and choose to live life God's way, and not the old way that I was used to if I was determined to keep my Fallen mask off. And it will most likely be the same for you. Because it took years for some of us to create the havoc in our lives by our bad choices, it's going to take a continual season of right choices to cut ties with old thinking patterns and belief systems.

Romans 12:2 tell us, "Don't copy the behavior and customs of this world, but let God transform you into a new person by changing the way you think. Then you will learn to know God's will for you, which is good and pleasing and perfect" (NLT).

Let God *transform* you! Changing into something different isn't easy. But if you stick with it and refuse to give up, like the butterfly that was once a worm, you will soon be flying free! Second Corinthians 5:17 promises, "Therefore, if anyone is in Christ, he is a new creation. The old has passed away; behold, the new has come" (ESV).

The Bible says we reap what we sow (Proverbs 11:18). I like that verse because it lets me know that if I keep doing the right thing, there will eventually be a right result.

———•———

Now that you are committed to walking this out, what's next? Get a Bible. Read it. Find out the eternal truth of God's Word and love for you. Be thankful for everything He has done for you daily. Repent when you've done wrong on a regular basis to keep your conscience clean. Pray and seek God's will and vision for your life. Find a good church that has great worship and sound teaching. Seek out fellowship with other believers and ask them to help you be accountable so that you don't drift back into your old life. Tell others about Jesus and what He has done for you. And when you are able, get busy giving back by serving others. Serving others shows that you are grateful for the miracle God has done, and it makes you joyful and happy!

Listen, money never made me happy anyway. The only thing people stole from me in my past was my ability to be full of greed and lust, not the ability to truly love with an abandoned heart. You see, I found out a long time ago that those people around me never really wanted me anyway; they only wanted to use me and my money. And as the old saying goes, money couldn't buy me love. You would think I would have figured this out after selling myself. I never dared to give my tricks my love; I only used them for their money. Let me shoot it to you straight . . . real talk. Money will never love you back no matter how hard you try to make it. It will never be there for you while you're in jail, be your doctor when you are sick, hug you when all your friends and family have rejected you, or be able to save your life if you're dying. Only Jesus can do that.

I don't know where I would be right now had I not surrendered my life to God. I'd probably be lying somewhere in a sleazy motel room, shooting up and turning tricks while my body fell apart, or in a hospital bed dying of a disease, or lying in an alley somewhere dead. What I do know is that today I am truly alive. I am finally home. I am set free. I am chosen. I have a purpose. I am ready for anything. I believe God will use everything for His good. Look again, my friend; it says it in His Word: "And we know that God causes everything to work together for the good of those who love God and are called according to his purpose for them" (Romans 8:28 NLT). Look, if you are still breathing, it is proof it's not over yet!

I dare you to take a chance on God and let Him radically and miraculously change your life. I dare you to step out into the unknown and fully trust Him to shape your life for the perfect and unique destiny that He has designed just for you. Trust me. It's worth the journey, however painful it may be! Because on the other side are His radical blessings!

My life will never be the same. Today I am a fisher of women who are drowning in the dark waters of the sex industry. And

I have no regrets. In fact, I'm glad I've been through what I've been through; it's made me who I am today. Pretty crazy, right? And that's why I believe I'm doing exactly what God had planned for me.

I finally decided to take off my Fallen mask and reveal to the world my real name: Annie, which means *grace*. My middle name, Laurie, is a form of Laura, which is derived from the Latin *laurus* (laurel, an evergreen shrub or tree whose leaves were woven into wreaths by the ancient Greeks to crown victors in various contests). My name essentially means grace with a crown of victory. And I open my arms and receive it!

Fallen is no more, for I have fallen into the arms of my Savior and I am finally home. The ironic thing is that Fallen means *grandchild of the ruler*, with the spiritual connotation of *Heir*. So even in my sin, God was calling me His heir and His grandchild.

God waits for you today, dear reader, to heal you, to redeem you, and to set you free. What are you waiting for?

CHAPTER 11

FREED TO SET OTHERS FREE

"I freed a thousand slaves. I could have freed a thousand
more if only they knew they were slaves."
—Harriet Tubman

In order for anyone to truly heal, we need to let God reveal the truth about the root of each issue we struggle with. The truth about ourselves is what sets us free more than anything else. When I was a slave to the sex industry, my perspective had to shift of how I viewed my life in order for me see that I needed to be freed from bondage.

After what Jesus had done for me, I wanted to offer that same hope to others. How could I not? It would be so selfish to keep it all to myself! I became a very eager student of wanting to give this freedom to others. Many times I wanted to jump out into the world and start a full-time ministry. But God would gently whisper in my ear, "Not yet, Annie. I want more time with you alone. Healing takes time. I want you to be ready and equipped for the journey ahead. You can't help others effectively if you still need help yourself. Focus on My love to heal you first. " One of my favorite scriptures that ministered to me and stopped me from jumping too far ahead of my healing was Psalm 46:10: "Be still, and know that I am God." I camped on that one, especially when I was tempted to jump ahead in my own timing. And trust me, that was often!

But God kept speaking to me and encouraging me, showing me things that prompted me to continue following in the direction He wanted me to go. As I studied the book of John, I read about Jesus during the Last Supper when He washed His disciples' feet, and it touched the very core of my being. Jesus taught the disciples at the Last Supper to give thanks for the breaking of bread, which represented His body, and the drinking of wine, which represented His blood, and signified the sacrifice He was about to become for all mankind to save them from their sins. Not only was He showing that He was willing to give up His life for His disciples, He was showing them how to be truly thankful for the pain and brokenness that was necessary in order for them to be redeemed.

What I took away from this event was Jesus' reminder to us as His followers to always be thankful to God—no matter what incredibly difficult thing He is asking us to do for Him. It signified to me how painful ministry can be, and that we need to always remember that going through the pain is so worth it because on the other side of death is a resurrected life! Many times in ministry we must sacrifice our time, energy, money, and pride to help someone else out of the pit of despair. And it will especially hurt and humble us when we help someone who ends up betraying us. Jesus knew Judas was going to betray Him, but He still chose to wash Judas' feet as an act of servanthood.

Here was Jesus at the Last Supper, knowing that He was about to be crucified, washing His disciples' dirty feet as a servant and not as Master. He could have been doing something else, like giving a final sermon to a huge crowd or performing a miracle in front of thousands of people. But He chose to do this very intimate, seemingly small and meaningless task behind closed doors. Because it wasn't about being seen or doing something amazing to go out with a bang; it was about the heart of being a servant, and loving someone enough to assist in cleaning the junk off of their lives—of being willing to get dirty for the sake of another. And not just people who are good to us, or people we are comfortable serving, like our friends, family, colleagues, etc. But the very ones others would reject—the Judases that we suspect and know have a plan to hurt us—we must clean their feet and be their servant too. We are never greater than the people we serve . . . ever!

> When he had finished washing their feet, he put on his clothes and returned to his place. "Do you understand what I have done for you?" he asked them. "You call me 'Teacher' and 'Lord,' and rightly so, for that is what I am. Now that I, your Lord and Teacher, have washed your feet, you also should wash one another's feet. I have set you an example that you should do as I have done for you. Very truly I tell you, no servant is greater than his master, nor is a messenger greater than the one who sent him. Now that you know these things, you will be blessed if you do them." (John 13:12–17)

Did you read that? We will be *blessed* if we serve! Why? Because when we bless others, He is faithful to take care of us in all our endeavors. Jesus says in Luke 18:29–30, "Truly I tell you . . . no one who has left home or wife or brothers or sisters or parents or children for the sake of the kingdom of God will fail to receive many times as much in this age, and in the age to come eternal life." And here's another reason why we serve: Ephesians 2:10 says, "For we are God's handiwork, created in Christ Jesus to do good works, which God prepared in advance for us to do." He *planned* for us to serve. And the most important reason I believe we serve is because we are so grateful for what He has done for us, that thankfulness compels us to want to give back to others.

This speaks volumes of passion, love, and leadership to my heart. I knew then that I had to go down to that Vegas Strip and reach out to the girls whom I knew God had called me to love and serve.

And it was scary at first. I even argued with God and told Him I thought He had asked the wrong person to do this task. After all, what would I say? Would they reject me? Would the pimps get angry and try to hurt me? God really spoke to me at this time and reminded me that I had been willing to risk my life for my pimp every time I knocked on a door and turned a trick—that I had risked my life every single night being a call girl. If I really and truly loved God, why wouldn't I do the same thing for Him? And He was right! True love risks its life for another, and like Jesus, love lays its very life down. I was crushed with tears of conviction and thankfulness, filled with a new passion and love for God in that moment of revelation, realizing that Jesus loved me enough to risk His life and die for me. I was overcome when I thought about what He had endured heading toward the cross—that He was beaten, flogged, maimed, spit on, rejected, ridiculed, and then nailed on that cross—just so that I could be alive, healed, and walk in freedom today.

Read Isaiah 53:7–12:

> He was oppressed and afflicted,
> > yet he did not open his mouth;
> he was led like a lamb to the slaughter,
> > and as a sheep before its shearers is silent,
> > so he did not open his mouth.
> By oppression and judgment he was taken away.
> > Yet who of his generation protested?
> For he was cut off from the land of the living;
> > for the transgression of my people he
> > > was punished.
> He was assigned a grave with the wicked,
> > and with the rich in his death,
> though he had done no violence,
> > nor was any deceit in his mouth.
>
> Yet it was the LORD's will to crush him and cause
> > him to suffer,
> > and though the LORD makes his life an
> > > offering for sin,
> he will see his offspring and prolong his days,
> > and the will of the LORD will prosper in
> > > his hand.
> After he has suffered,
> > he will see the light of life and be satisfied;

> *by his knowledge my righteous servant will*
> *justify many,*
> *and he will bear their iniquities.*
> *Therefore I will give him a portion among*
> *the great,*
> *and he will divide the spoils with the strong,*
> *because he poured out his life unto death,*
> *and was numbered with the transgressors.*
> *For he bore the sin of many,*
> *and made intercession for the transgressors.*

When I read this passage, I realized how much I could relate to Jesus, having been rejected, spit on, beaten, lied about, and left for dead many times by my pimp and the tricks who abused me. This was incredible to me, because Jesus truly understood my pain. And His pain He had to go through, already healed me! By His stripes, *we are healed*. What a gift! His very life! Why wouldn't I want to risk it all for another? It was time to trust God completely and step out in faith. Because if we can't live out the faith we profess, then is it real faith?

———•———

In the summer of 2005, armed with nothing but a stack of business cards listing my name and number, I started my first outreach ministry. Later that year I would name the ministry Hookers for Jesus. I hit the Strip, the line of upper-crust bars and casinos and hotels that I had once trekked, answering calls of greed, lust, and pleasure. Except this time I was no longer a call girl—I was answering God's call on my life.

And why wouldn't I? How could I hold this precious treasure I had been given as a gift all to myself? That would be so selfish!

It was easy to spot the working girls. I had been one of them, after all. I knew the coy, confident looks, the trips up and down elevators. This was my town. I had once run the streets as one of the most successful high-class call girls. I knew about lust. I knew about greed. I knew about pockets full of money. I knew about violence. I knew about the pull of pimps. But now I knew the remedy for the sickness of all those things—God's love.

I approached the women discreetly. With a big smile on my face, I quietly told them, "My name is Annie. I sold my body for years. I know what it's like to almost lose your soul. I want you to know that God has a better plan for you. You don't have to be a slave to a pimp. You don't have to sell your body. God loves you." I never forced Jesus on them. I just shared how my life had been radically changed.

Some of the women were nice, chatting with me for a few minutes before they hauled themselves off to work. Some cried and would eventually take up my offer of coming to church with me. Some were insulted at my insinuations and vehemently denied selling their bodies, even though I witnessed them solicit random men.

I did these outreaches every few weeks and started bringing girls off the street to church with me. I even let some of them stay with me temporarily and put others up in a motel with the money my pastor (Ron Vietti) graciously donated to my emerging ministry. But there were so many women being sex trafficked! And there was never enough room. I felt a burning desire in my heart to start a home for working girls who wanted to get out of the game, to provide a way out, an escape from their violent pimps. When my life turned around, I was blessed to be in a safe environment to grow as a person and heal from my past. I wanted to do the same for other women.

A few months earlier I became involved with Valley Bible Fellowship and continued my street outreaches with their support, eventually founding the organization Hookers for Jesus. Did you know the word *hooker* doesn't just mean a sex worker? It represents a clipper-style boat from the 1600s made for fishing. *Hooker* also means a "fish hook." I'm tired of people thinking that *hooker* is a dirty word, so I sought to take the name back for God. Jesus said, "Follow Me, and I will make you fishers of men" (Matthew 4:19 NKJV). I am following His lead and casting my line and hook to catch people to hear about the love of Jesus and receive the message of salvation and grace. My passion is to help prostitutes, pimps, and strippers—anyone, really, in the sex trade—to see that there is an abundant life waiting for them to finally live outside of the sex industry.

Pastors Ron Vietti and Jim Crews were so supportive of what I was doing, and they lovingly opened their arms to all the girls that were coming out of sex trafficking and prostitution. They sincerely understood that these are the women that Jesus defended, hung around with, and loved, and were very supportive of my efforts to reach these ladies and show them that they are loved no matter what.

In 2006, a local CBS newscaster George Knapp got in touch with me and asked for a story. Honestly, I didn't want to do it at first. But I knew that I had to obey what God was leading me to do, so I prayed about it. A couple of months later I finally relented. After the piece aired, I started getting recognition on social media. My good friend Heather Veitch, founder of JC's Girls (a forerunner and first ministry to go into strip clubs), and I joined forces in a simple media project posting our videos on YouTube. I was also writing blogs on MySpace, then the most-visited social networking site in the world, and my pieces at times were ranked number one on their site.

Doors started opening left and right. You know that it's God moving on your behalf when people are calling you and contacting you that you never thought knew who you were! I had no manager for all these requests, yet the offers to speak and be interviewed kept flooding in. Schools, law enforcement, churches, radio stations, television venues, all inviting me to speak about awareness and my story. More doors started flying open. Through MySpace, Christian recording artist Carmen connected with me and asked if I could share my story on TBN. More media appearances followed, including a riveting debate on *Nightline* with pastor and author Mark Driscoll and Dr. Deepak Chopra talking about the question "Is Satan Real?" (Um, yeah . . . he sure is!) Then more national TV specials and documentaries ensued, including an *I Am Second* film (www.iamsecond.com/seconds/annie-lobert); *Nefarious: Merchant of Souls* (Exodus Cry); and an Investigation Discovery Channel's documentary called "Hookers Saved on the Strip."

At the heart of Hookers for Jesus was the idea of opening a home for sex workers leaving the sex-trafficking industry. After a few fits and starts, Destiny House opened in 2008. Today, our ministry, Hookers for Jesus, runs various ministries in addition to Destiny House. We offer a program called Saturday Night Love, an outreach ministry on the Strip; Ladies of Destiny, weekly Bible study classes for the women in and outside our home for self-improvement and education; K.I.S.S. (Keeping Innocent Sisters Safe), our jail outreach, education, and sex-trafficking awareness program; Diamonds and Pearls, an outreach focused on strip clubs; and Grace Chicks, to mentor and transport girls when they need rides.

Had there been a ministry such as ours when I was trapped in sex trafficking, I might have been rescued a lot earlier and spared much of the suffering I experienced. But at the same time, I do believe that it was meant to be—that God would eventually take what was evil and ugly and turn it into something beautiful for His glory.

CHAPTER 12

MY DREAM COME TRUE

*"If you keep on believing,
the dreams that you wish will come true."*
—Cinderella

As I forged forward in my life, my focus fixed in the right direction, taking slow and steady steps toward my purpose, moving deeper into my faith, I still wondered about love. I was a hopeless romantic. The Disney fairy tale was still in the back of my mind, but not as an ideal I had to strive for. I just believed with all my heart that there was someone out there specifically that God had in mind for me. You know . . . the "one."

While I no longer looked at my past with paralyzing regret, I couldn't ignore the obvious—a string of failed and often toxic relationships. Nor could I ignore the beautiful truth that with God everything is redeemable. *Everything!* I held on to that hope for dear life.

I tread carefully as I prayed and dated, working out the artful balance of being open but guarded. I had been through a lot and was cautious around men. I didn't want to be victim to bitterness or resentment or to sabotage relationships because of my past. I love what C. S. Lewis wrote in his book *The Four Loves*:

> *To love at all is to be vulnerable. Love anything and your heart will be wrung and possibly broken. If you want to make sure of keeping it intact you must give it to no one. . . . Wrap it carefully round with hobbies and little luxuries; avoid all entanglements. Lock it up safe in the casket or coffin of your selfishness. But in that casket, safe, dark, motionless, airless, it will change. It will not be broken; it will become unbreakable, impenetrable, irredeemable. To love is to be vulnerable.*

Sure, I made some serious mistakes along the way and had my heart broken in the process, even as a Christian woman. No one is perfect! My heart still longed for someone. As painful as it was in the process of trusting God, I kept on trusting Him with all my heart. I leaned into learning more and more about how a man of God who truly loved me was supposed to treat me.

I will never forget the showdown I had with God. I was lying in bed one night, praying for God to reveal to me the plan He had for me, when I heard a still, small voice say, "I will not send you the right husband until you understand who you are in Me and what it's like to be a godly wife. I want to be your husband first so I can show you how your earthly husband should treat you." Frankly, these weren't the words I wanted to hear. But I submitted to the process, and I cried long and hard that night, asking Jesus to comfort me with His presence. That night I felt His loving arms around me as I slept. The next few months I dove in to letting God lead me like He was my husband, falling more deeply in love with His gentle, kind, and patient demeanor.

It was truly a sweet romantic time in my life—one that I will never forget because I became so close to Jesus. In the process I found out more deeply who I was in Christ, and that my identity didn't need to be tied to finding a husband to complete His plan. He could still use me regardless, and I told God, "Look, God, if I have to be a nun for the rest of my life, that is fine with me." As soon as I said it, I couldn't believe those words had come out of my mouth, because I was feisty when it came to being determined to get my way.

But God knew that about me, so when I surrendered it and meant it, He led me to read relationship books on godly marriage. And what did a godly marriage look like? Here is what I believed I needed in order to know that my future husband was the "one" for me:

1. He needed to love God with all his heart, mind, body, and soul. God needed to absolutely be first in his life.
2. He needed to be a provider. If we were to be married, he needed to be willing to truly be my husband by providing for me financially if I couldn't and be willing to take care of me if I was sick.
3. He needed to have the ability to defend and protect me in any given situation—dangerous or not.
4. He needed to be willing to take a bullet for me. In other words, like Jesus, he would be willing to die for me in

order that I may live. He would have to be man enough to want to save my life if it came down to it.

5. He needed to be a true gentleman who was willing to wait to have sexual relations until after we were married. A man who truly loves you will not compromise your sexuality by expecting to sample your body like a piece of merchandise. I knew that the true "one" God would send me would never force something on me sexually that I wasn't ready to do, and if he tried to, that would give me an indication that he wasn't the gentleman God planned for me.

I will have to admit, being who I am and the type of comfort romantically that I felt I needed, that last one was going to be difficult. In fact, in 2005, I slept with someone I met and got engaged to. He told me I was going to be his wife, and then he broke my heart. So when I said I made mistakes, I meant it. Look, ladies, don't believe that someone is going to be your husband just because he claims God told him he was. Don't fall for it. You never really know someone until you've spent a lot of time with him and dated him for a while. He will always eventually show his true character. Don't play their victim!

When I look back at this time in my life, I understand the inner healing God needed to do in my heart. I had to learn about healthy relationships. I had to learn about biblical marriage. I needed to understand that God desired me to be committed to Him as my husband first in order for me to understand true commitment to someone else. It's very beautiful, the way God romances us and gives us the desires of our hearts. Especially when we have been out in the desert for so long looking for pools of water that are not there.

God continued to bring to my mind one of my now-favorite scriptures in Proverbs 18:22: "He who finds a wife finds what is good and receives favor from the Lord." Through these words, God was reminding me that I didn't need to play the harlot and chase after a man. That was the old me. Fallen. I needed to be a dignified lady and wait patiently. So I stayed still before God, faithful in prayer, believing God's plan for a husband. It wasn't about me any longer. It wasn't about my plans, my desires, my wants, my dreams, my hopes. It was about aligning myself with God's plans for me. There comes a time in our lives where we really need to grow up and not force the doors open that God doesn't want open. Doing that is nothing short of manipulation, which really is a form of witchcraft! (Ouch! That might hurt some of you like it did me at one point!)

And then it happened . . .

In June 2007, my good friend Heather, the founder of JC's Girls, the first strip club ministry of its kind, had dinner one night with one of her friends, Kevin Max, of the Christian pop bands Audio Adrenalin and (formerly) with DC Talk, when Oz Fox, founding member and lead guitarist of the Christian metal band Stryper, showed up and joined the table.

Heather called me as soon as she came home that night. "Annie, I just met your future husband," she gushed with excitement as she told me about Oz and how my name had come up in the dinner conversation.

I laughed, skeptical. "Oh, shut up. You did not!"

Heather didn't back down. "I sure did, I sure did! I swear to you, girl, you are going to marry this guy."

It sounded crazy, and while I wasn't convinced, I'll admit, I wondered, *Could it be? Maybe?*

Oz messaged me on MySpace that very night via e-mail. He told me he admired what I was doing and that he'd love to meet me sometime. I'll have to admit, at first I was cautious and skeptical of him. Come on, he was a rock star! Most rock stars are womanizers. There was no way I was going through that again! Regardless, curiosity got the best of me, and I was intrigued, clicking on his profile to see what he was doing in life and his rock music career. I was blown away by his profile and his guitar talent. We e-mailed several times, and while he continued to invite me to see a couple of his shows, life happened. He was busy traveling on tour with Stryper. I was busy doing outreach work and building our Hookers for Jesus ministry (see the back of the book for more information) and couldn't find the right time to connect in person, although I really wanted to.

Finally, in February 2008, I took Oz up on his invitation and showed up at one of his local shows with a friend of mine. We hung out after the show and had an amazing time. I remember him taking a bunch of pictures with me and thinking, *Oh my goodness, this guy is crushing on me!* I liked Oz. He was talented, laid-back, funny, and good-looking. The next morning he asked me out for a pancake breakfast, but I couldn't go. Oz later told me he was disappointed and assumed I was blowing him off, which was the furthest thing from the truth. What really happened was that I was in my pajamas when he called me, and I needed an hour to get ready so I would look good for him. He couldn't wait because of his schedule, and he needed to drive back to LA. We continued to exchange e-mails and texts after that, but didn't see each other for a while. I was traveling quite a bit, speaking and doing ministry, and he was on tour with Stryper again.

I continued to seek God and pray, wondering if perhaps Oz was the man for me. Secretly I wanted it to be true, but I wasn't stupid. I knew not to push the issue. I wanted to keep being obedient about what God told me. Then it happened.

Oz was playing a concert in Vegas on October 25, 2008, and he invited me and a friend. He asked us to dress up as the venue, the Hilton, was throwing a glitzy Halloween party later that night. I panicked. I didn't have anything to wear, so I did the best I could donning an old outfit from my club days and some spiked heels. I probably looked a little too sexy for a Christian gal. But honestly, at this point, I didn't care. When I walked into the ballroom of the hotel where Oz would be playing in a few minutes, I think his eyes almost popped out of his head. He immediately came over and hugged me. That did it! I felt a wave of supernatural connection that I knew was real. After the show we went to a romantic late-night restaurant, sat by a glowing fire, and talked for hours. *This could be serious.*

After that night, we were pretty much inseparable. Our phone conversations lasted for hours on end. I couldn't wait to talk to him and see him on the weekends when he would come into town to play with his band and visit. The more we got to know each other, the more I liked him. This was getting dangerous. My heart was on fire.

Unlike other guys I was interested in, I didn't chase Oz. He pursued me, slowly and unrelentingly, like a perfect gentleman. We had a wild romance. For the first time in my life, I was falling in love with a man who wasn't trying to get into my pants or push the relationship somewhere I didn't want it to go, physically or otherwise. Oz courted me in a godly way. He wasn't intimidating; he was loving. He wasn't aggressive; he was patient. He wasn't demanding; he was kind. Oz became my best friend and confidant. He encouraged me to walk in my calling without feeling threatened. He respected my ministry and supported me fully.

Years earlier, as I prayed for a husband, I would have visions of this mystery person. He was muscular and had long hair, and many times my mind would capture images of this person mowing a lawn. When Oz sent me a picture of him mowing the lawn one day, I knew he was the one God had destined for me. (And yes, he has long hair too! He is in a metal band, after all!)

There were times I wanted to discuss marriage, but every time that desire came up, God told me to keep quiet. Oh, you don't know how hard that was! I needed to be still and submit to the process He wanted to orchestrate. A few months into our relationship, Oz asked me what kind of diamonds I liked, to which I happily replied, "Heart shaped!"

On Valentine's Day in 2009, Oz gave me a dozen each of beautiful red, white, and pink roses and took me to a romantic Mexican restaurant where a mariachi band played for us tableside. I was convinced that at any moment my man was going to propose. The band played a few songs, our meal came and went, and when Oz paid the bill without even a mention of the word *marriage*, I felt disappointed.

As we drove home, he said, "Let's have some dessert at the Fireside Grill." Forty-five minutes later we were sitting in front of a cozy fire, eating chocolate cheesecake, and listening to a jazz guitarist strum romantic melodies, when Oz got down on his knee and finally popped the question.

"Will you marry me?" he asked with a bright-red face, flashing a picture on his cell phone of a heart-shaped diamond engagement ring that was in the process of being made for me.

My heart flooded with joy. "Of course!" I shouted, right before I gave him a playful shove. "I'm going to kick your butt, Oz. You waited till almost midnight!" We got married four months later, on June 5, broadcasting our wedding live on the Internet. I walked down the aisle that day with my tearful father at my side, who gave me away to my true knight in shining armor. As Dad and I slowly made the emotional walk down the white carpet, Oz serenaded me with a touching song written by his good friend Wade Haynes.

I walked down that aisle a virgin in Christ, in a beautiful, sparkling wedding dress, crowned with a tiara of diamonds— just like a real princess. And on this day I also became a mother when I gained three children through Oz: Paul, twenty-seven, Lea, twenty-five, and Tara, twenty. We all get along great. I love them dearly, and I feel like I have known them forever! And remember my early dream of wanting to be in the music business? By being Oz's wife, I get to be a part of his career. I work hard to support him in his music and am also producing songs with him that we have written together. You see, friend, God knew what He was doing! He truly does know the desires of our hearts.

Dear friend, I found my once-upon-a-time fairy tale. And it wasn't because of any plan I forced or design I created. It was because I surrendered to what God wanted for my life. Do you see what can happen if you truly trust His plan for your life? If we just stop fighting God and holding on to what we think we need in our lives, He will give us the desires of our hearts.

Our marriage is certainly not perfect and it comes with its share of challenges, but there is no doubt in my mind that Oz is the husband I need, want, love, and am continually excited to spend the rest of my life with. And the best part is, he is also my confidant and best friend.

Is it crazy that a man can love and marry a former harlot? Maybe. But to me, it's just another incredible example of how God will redeem everything if we are willing to trust and believe in Him.

APPENDIX A

WHAT IS SEX TRAFFICKING?

When I first started doing outreaches on the Las Vegas Strip, I had no idea what *sex trafficking* was. Here's what the U.S. Department of State says about sex trafficking in an article titled "What Is Trafficking in Persons?" found on their Web site:

> When an adult is coerced, forced, or deceived into prostitution—or maintained in prostitution through coercion—that person is a victim of trafficking. All of those involved in recruiting, transporting, harboring, receiving, or obtaining the person for that purpose have committed a trafficking crime. Sex trafficking can also occur within debt bondage, as women and girls are forced to continue in prostitution through the use of unlawful "debt" purportedly incurred through their transportation, recruitment, or even their crude "sale," which exploiters insist they must pay off before they can be free.

It is critical to understand that a person's initial consent to participate in prostitution is not legally determinative; if an individual is thereafter held in service through psychological manipulation or physical force, that person is a trafficking victim and should receive the benefits outlined in the United Nations' Palermo Protocol and applicable laws.

Human trafficking is considered modern-day slavery. Right now in the world there are approximately twelve million to twenty-seven million slaves who are currently trapped in this atrocity.

I didn't know I was actually a victim of sex trafficking until years afterward. I just knew I was a former high-class prostitute. Sure, I knew I had been severely abused by my boyfriend/pimp, but I assumed it was my fault and my choice. I never considered myself a victim, let alone a victim of sex trafficking. But by these definitions, *I clearly was.*

Please remember that when a woman is referred to as a prostitute and is being pimped, the correct term is *sex-trafficking victim* (victim of commercial sexual exploitation). A woman who is pimped is most likely not able to leave her pimp unless she dies or goes into hiding (i.e., the witness protection program). Most sex-trafficking victims believe they deserve the torture they receive through beatings and verbal abuse, which pimps use to manipulate them and destroy their self-worth.

Many people don't see or can't understand the battle women face when they are manipulated into being a sex slave. The combination of physical, emotional, verbal, and psychological abuse results in an unhealthy pull toward, and dependency on, their pimp. In the next few pages, I will give you a glimpse into the mentality that drives the pimp game so you can understand the power and depth of the brainwashing involved.

There are many different situations in which a girl or young lady becomes a victim of sex trafficking. There are true, heartbreaking accounts of individuals all over the world being kidnapped right out of their homes and forced to have sex in another part of the world. Some are even sold by their families. And, yes, there is a percentage of females who willingly enter the game and purposely continue to remain in it. Frankly, I strongly believe that percentage is a small one. Many sex workers want desperately to get out but believe—due to threats and violence—that they cannot escape.

———•———

A typical potential sex-trafficking victim will often be approached by a pimp with a charming personality (a knight in shining armor type) who will start out acting like her boyfriend, just like Julian. Ultimately, these tactics are used for control and manipulation to keep her believing that she will lose the love she fantasizes he has for her if she doesn't do what he demands. Psychologically she is tricked into thinking that the pimp loves her, will protect her, and will take care of her for the rest of her life. In reality, pimps are masters of manipulation through verbal, mental, and severe physical abuse. A sex worker is kept in a submissive position at all times to sell her body for sex to make the pimp rich. She gives all her money to the pimp, and if she leaves, she will most likely leave with *nothing but the clothes on her back.*

There are so many ways that a pimp overpowers and controls his sex worker so she feels helpless and hopeless. (But first, let me say that pimps are not always men.) I want to offer a few of them:

- He separates and isolates her from friends and family.
- He keeps track of and total control over her every move.
- He puts her in unfamiliar geographic locations as she works for him.
- He learns a victim's insecurities over time to later exploit.
- He takes away a victim's identification, money, assets, and access to money, forcing her to be financially dependent on him.
- He uses physical torture like beatings, rape, forced drug use, or denial of food or access to a bathroom.
- He vacillates between cycles of affection and violence.
- He harms another person in the stable (a.k.a. polygamy pimp family) as punishment for a victim's disobedience.
- He blackmails the victim and threatens her family members and friends.
- He uses sophisticated methods of manipulating the human desire to hope through false promises and lies about a future better life. Victims who are children are especially vulnerable to these false promises, as well as women who have been sexually or otherwise abused prior to meeting their trafficker.
- He will sometimes manipulate the victim's family with charm and try to buy their acceptance and pretend he is a lofty businessman taking care of their daughter.

- If she has a drug addiction, he uses drugs as a bargaining chip to manipulate her into working longer hours for him.
- He withholds affection and sex as a way to emotionally control her moods and her love for him.

You can get a feel above of how much emotional, psychological, and even physical manipulation the pimp exerts to keep his sex worker in the game. Now I want you to get a glimpse of the mind-set of a sex worker. You are probably wondering why women get into the sex industry/prostitution game and why victims stay as long as they do. As I mentioned earlier, there are a number of reasons why this may be the case, but I want to highlight a variety of both physical and psychological reasons.

- Victims often have a romantic relationship with their traffickers and are in love with them; to them, a loss of love would equal a loss of self-worth and value.
- Many sex workers are held captive and cannot physically leave their environment.
- In many trafficking networks, victims are watched 24/7.
- Sex workers live in fear of being beaten, killed, arrested, and having their loved ones harmed.
- Victims carry an overwhelming amount of shame about some of the sex acts they have been forced to perform. They may also blame themselves for being foolish to get involved in the circumstances they find themselves in. These self-blaming activities are often used by pimps to manipulate the sex workers.

- In many trafficking cases, victims have shown widely researched behaviors of traumatic bonding similar to the Stockholm syndrome.
- Pimps often brainwash their victims into thinking law enforcement is the enemy and is out to get them.
- In the face of extreme control, violence, and captivity, many sex workers give up hope and become resigned to their circumstances.
- Some victims are not aware of available support networks or resources that may help them get out of their situation.
- Some do not self-identify as victims of human trafficking. Many believe that because they chose the lifestyle of prostitution they should not be considered sex-traffic victims. They may be unaware of the elements of the crime or the legal protection available to them.

When sex-trafficking victims endure such severe levels of trauma, physical abuse, and psychological manipulation, many end up normalizing the abuse. This is actually proven in post-traumatic stress disorder studies of brain scans of victims with PTSD.

A colleague of mine, Dr. Halleh Seddighzadeh, is a forensic traumatologist and counter-trafficking expert. I attended one of her trauma trainings, and she shared that oftentimes, sex-trafficking victims endure such repeated and severe levels of physical trauma and psychological abuse that their brains end up normalizing the abuse. She explained that the brain physically changes as a result of the interpersonal experience of trauma. In other words, traumatic stress anatomically changes the structure of the brain. Dr. Seddighzadeh presented slides of brain scans in post-traumatic stress disorder (PTSD) studies, revealing how the victims of PTSD actually had physical changes to their brains.

For sex workers, what may have once been deemed violent or manipulative behavior is now a regular part of life. As a result, the victim feels helpless and hopeless and believes no one can help her, a feeling that is continually reinforced by her pimp.

Sex workers suffer from a number of psychological disorders, mental health issues, substance abuse and addictions, and physical consequences. These include post-traumatic stress disorder. Melissa Farley of ProstitutionResearch.com says research shows that 70 percent of former prostitutes develop it—and this is the very same rate as war veterans. Other conditions for sex workers may include depression, anxiety, eating disorders, panic attacks, dissociative disorders, schizophrenia, developmental disorders, social phobia, mood disorders, insomnia, and obsessive-compulsive disorder.

I empathize with many victims of sex trafficking and former prostitutes as I, like many of those I serve, have walked through the dark valleys of PTSD, depression, severe anxiety, addiction, and mood swings. The internal and external pain that is endured as a result of this lifestyle is heartbreaking.

TESTIMONIALS FROM DESTINY HOUSE

While all the ministries are near and dear to my heart, Destiny House is particularly precious to me. Through this safe haven, I have been extremely blessed to meet so many women whose lives have been radically transformed through God's love and power.

What these women have been through is gut-wrenching and heartbreaking. But there is nothing that the power of God's love cannot heal or make whole. We teach these women that their lives in slavery can be unchained so they can live freely. Once they experience this, they understand that they are accepted and embraced by the love of God, no matter what their past looks like. These women bring joy to my heart every day, and I am grateful that I have the opportunity to work with them and to personally witness their transformation. It's not easy. It takes courage. It takes honesty. And it takes a lot of serious, hard work. But I am committed. I'm so proud of them. And I love them with all my heart.

In more ways than one, I understand their heartaches, fears, struggles, and pain. When they want to run away and go back to the sex industry, I get it. When they want to run back to their sex traffickers because they are in love, I can totally relate. I can reach them. I can show them that I once was lost, but now I'm found. I once was blind to my own prison of lies that I lived in, but Jesus has set me free. I once was trapped in an abusive past that I never thought I would escape from. I am living proof that the power of God is indeed alive, and if they believe, their lives can be redeemed too.

I want you to get a glimpse into the redemptive power of Jesus Christ through reading some of their stories in their own words.

> When I was a little girl, I had dreams of becoming a schoolteacher or even a basketball player. But those dreams suddenly vanished at the age of seven when I started being sexually abused by my family members. By the time I turned fifteen, I was dating men old enough to be my father. And when I turned eighteen, I was being sex trafficked by a man I thought loved me. Because of my age and vulnerability, I was easily manipulated into the life of prostitution. By the time I turned twenty, I had been through things no young adult should ever have to endure. I didn't have any good guidance in my life. I lost all hope, degraded myself, and couldn't see a bright future. Then I found out about Hookers for Jesus and eventually moved

into Destiny House. I've been living here for six months now, learning and healing and discovering amazing things about God, myself, and the future I want to have. Because of the grace of God I have been renewed, redeemed, and allowed to start my life over again.

—*Tyricka, 23*

While I had hopes and dreams for my life, I became a teen mom, a teen wife, and then a teen stripper. After nine years in an on-and-off dysfunctional marriage full of abuse and infidelity on both sides and giving birth to two more kids by two different men, I found myself divorced, a prostitute, using drugs, giving my money to pimps, and ultimately had to give up custody of my three kids to my abusive ex-husband. I met a man named Eric, who would later become my husband, and he helped me realize I needed Jesus. But I still struggled and could not escape my life as a prostitute, going back into it for different reasons. I finally discovered Destiny House, where I am receiving counseling and, most important, am growing in Christ and gaining knowledge and wisdom of God's Word. Although this is the most difficult thing I have done because I am away from my family, I know God brought me here for His reason and purpose. I expect to be prepared to be a better mom and a better wife and a better woman for society, equipped with better life skills and job skills and fully prepared to fulfill God's will for my life.

—*Amy, 40*

I was once lost, trapped in human trafficking from the ages of fourteen to thirty. As a teenage runaway, a pimp tricked me into working in a brothel in the Deep South. Far out in the country, it was a locked, heavily guarded facility. I endured months of being "broke," which entailed severe beating, and sometimes being chained to a bed and forced to service customers. Eventually I became mentally conditioned and resigned that this was to be my life. I stayed in the game for fifteen years under the control of three different pimps. The year I turned thirty, I decided I couldn't live another day like this. I ran away and went home to my family. I quickly married and gave birth to my beautiful children, pushing all the trauma and pain deep down inside. Eventually it manifested itself into addictions, which I fought for years. Over and over I would get my life together, and then the pain of my past would surface and I'd tear the good stuff down. Then I met Annie and got the opportunity to come to Destiny House. Since being here I have been able to work through my demons and embrace the love that Christ has for me. Through the work I'm doing here, I have hope for my future because it is now being built on the foundation of God.

—*Tina, 49*

Our ministry has helped women from all lifestyles, not just sex workers. Read the following testimonies of women to see some of their struggles.

I grew up in a very broken and angry home. For years I did everything I could to kill the pain. I was addicted to drugs and men, prostituting myself to dealers to feed my addiction. I didn't care what I took or who I slept with. One night I went to a party and was handed a random pill, and I took it without asking what it was. I vaguely recall being raped by multiple men, and the next day I was horrified and ashamed . . . but even more, I was angry. I went deeper into my addiction.

One day I was driving and smoking weed when I was pulled over and arrested. As I sat in jail, I remember being so scared and praying to God a deep, gut-wrenching prayer for help. It was there that I felt peace for the first time in my life. I didn't know how or why or what it meant, but it was strong. I knew I was done with the life; I just wanted out.

After I got out of jail, I went to college overseas and came back to the States to attend a Discipleship Training school with Youth With

A Mission (YWAM) and eventually joining its staff. I felt like God had really given me a heart to disciple women, specifically sex-trafficked women. I led an outreach to Thailand and was going to seminars in Vegas and researching trafficking when I heard Annie Lobert speak and tell her story. After my commitment with YWAM was completed, I was able to join the staff of Hookers for Jesus, where I am now the program coordinator.

God's plan has been so much more beautiful than mine ever was. He took all of the hard things I went through and has used my mistakes for His glory. I thank God every day for this blessing and that He is Lord!

—*Sami, 30*

My father started sexually abusing me when I was six. I repressed this for decades and, looking back, I know that a lot of my fears and issues I have faced stem from the childhood abuse. I was a virgin when I graduated from high school. But I was sick and tired of being a good girl and not having boyfriends. I became promiscuous from that point on until March 1977 when I got saved. I promised myself I would save myself for marriage. Then the guy who was my first love, now my ex-husband, came back into my life on Christmas Eve of 1977. He broke down my resistance, and I ended up giving myself to him sexually the following year. It wasn't until we were married in June 1979 that I realized he was a porn and sex addict. I tried to be what he wanted and do what he wanted for decades before I finally decided to leave him in 2011.

I met Annie shortly after that and then started volunteering with Hookers for Jesus in 2012, working on the financial side of the ministry. I am now the director of operations for Hookers for Jesus, as well as a board member for the ministry. I also serve at porn conventions alongside Annie and my church's Naked Truth ministry. God has used Hookers for Jesus to deeply heal me. I have learned that my ex-husband's porn and sex addiction, and that all of the money we spent, was really supporting sex trafficking and sexual exploitation. The women we work with who were trafficked initially assume that I am some middle-aged white woman who is clueless about what they have been through. Now I have earned the nickname of "Gangster Carol."

—*Carol, 56*

You don't have to sell yourself for money to be a prostitute. I grew up in a Christian home. I went to church every Sunday and was involved in various church groups, and I loved it. I believed in God and had accepted Jesus into my heart. I grew up knowing "the right thing to do." Even though I grew up knowing it was wrong to have sex before marriage, I still messed up.

I started dating a guy who eventually told me he wanted to marry me. When I found out he was addicted to pornography, I was devastated. My confidence had turned to insecurity. We started sleeping together, and I tried to rationalize it because I thought it was better for him to be with me than to be looking at porn, and besides, we were going to get married anyway. I was giving him sex in exchange for his love and attention, and that's prostitution. And because he continued to look at porn, I felt betrayed, angry, and worthless. I made a decision to stop sleeping with him, and two weeks later he broke up with me.

I did not start forgiving myself or feeling better about myself until one night when I heard Annie speaking at a Ladies of Destiny class about Jesus and the Samaritan woman at the well. Hearing that story, I knew I was that woman, and I realized that Jesus still loves me. He still loves me even though I messed up, even though I knew better. I thank God for His grace and mercy, and I thank Annie and Hookers for Jesus for reminding me that I am still loved.

—*Janessa, 21*

ACKNOWLEDGMENTS

To the Worthy Publishing team: Thank you for taking a chance on a story like mine, which many did not have the guts to risk telling. Your choice to publish my memoir shows courage, strength, and boldness . . . but most of all volumes of love for a girl who had once lost her way.

To the Fedd Agency: Esther Fedorkevich, we did it! Finally finished the book that I know God called me to pen. Ever since I met you in 2006, I knew our paths would cross again. I am so glad they did in 2011 and that you kept the fighting spirit alive when publishing doors kept closing on us. You made this so worth the journey in believing that God can do anything through those who believe. I love you. And, Lisa, thank you for all your encouragement, for being my cheerleader on the sidelines telling me to keep going.

To A. J. Gregory: What can I say, my fellow warrior writer? It has been an amazing and incredible journey with you, whether we were pushing through painful moments or celebrating God's deliverance, mercy, and grace. Thanks for helping me map out my story and making my words colorful and alive. You have been a wonderful mentor and amazing friend in helping me visualize my journey to the beautiful kingdom of forgiveness.

ABOUT THE AUTHOR

Annie Lobert is a survivor of more than a decade of sex trafficking. She worked as an exotic dancer and a high-class escort and was prostituted in Hawaii, Minneapolis, and Las Vegas.

And because of her experience, she has become known as an internationally recognized expert and advocate of ministry to men and women in the commercial sex industry.

In 2005 Annie established Hookers for Jesus, a nonprofit ministry that reaches out to ladies in Las Vegas who are prostitutes/sex trafficking victims so they can share the gospel of Jesus Christ with them and help them escape the lifestyle in which they're trapped. Part of their ministry includes Destiny House, a safe haven for women who wish to leave their pasts behind but have no place to go.

Annie has been featured on national broadcasts: *Dr. Drew's Lifechangers*, *The Today Show*, *Nightline*, *Joy Behar*, *The Tyra Banks Show*, *Joyce Meyer*, *Life Today*, *Help Line TV*, *The 700 Club*, *The Jim Bakker Show*, TBNs *Praise the Lord*, an *I Am Second* film, as well as an upcoming MSNBC series titled *Sex Slaves in America*.

Additionally, Annie filmed a three-part TV mini docu-series on the Investigation Discovery channel called *Hookers Saved on the Strip*, which features three ladies who were rescued by her. This series can now be found on Netflix.

Annie has been heard on radio programs and interviewed in major news publications across the nation and world: The Associated Press, the *New York Post*, *LA Times*, *Penthouse*, and *Charisma* magazine.

Annie speaks for governmental organizations, judicial offices, police force trainings, educational systems, community groups, and churches to educate and assist others to action regarding rescuing people from prostitution and sex trafficking.

When Annie is taking time off from her busy schedule, she spends it with her husband, Oz Fox, who is a founding member and current guitarist and vocalist for the heavy metal band Stryper.

ABOUT HOOKERS FOR JESUS

"Jesus called out to them: 'Come follow me, and I will show you how to fish for people!'"
—Matthew 4:19 (NLT)

Hookers for Jesus is a nonprofit organization that addresses the harmful effects of prostitution, sex trafficking, and sexual exploitation linked to pornography and the sex industry.

Hook • Hope • Heal • Help

The primary mission of Hookers for Jesus is to Hook (outreach), Give Hope (Jesus), Heal (emotional & spiritual restoration), and Help (transitional assistance) those who have been negatively affected by sex trafficking and the adult entertainment industry.

Hookers for Jesus is committed to our community. We desire to encourage economic development as well as personal, academic, and professional growth in every individual affected by the abuses of commercial sexual exploitation. Our goals include providing human services opportunities leading to self-sufficiency apart from a life in the sex industry.

If you suspect that someone is being exploited, or if you are interested in Destiny House's twelve-month healing and recovery program for ladies eighteen and older coming out of sex trafficking and prostitution, please call **(702) 883-5155.**

You can also call the National Human Trafficking Resource Center hotline at 1-888-373-7888.

For more information about Hookers for Jesus or to seek more information on rescuing women from prostitution and sex trafficking, visit our Web site, **www.hookersforjesus.net**, or visit the **Hookers for Jesus Facebook Page**.

And if this book has changed your life, we would love to hear from you at **info@hookersforjesus.net**.

WORTHY
PUBLISHING

If you enjoyed this book, will you consider
sharing the message with others?

- Mention the book in a Facebook post, Twitter update, Pinterest pin, blog post, or upload a picture through Instagram.

- Recommend this book to those in your small group, book club, workplace, and classes.

- Head over to facebook.com/worthypublishing or facebook.com/hookersforjesus, "LIKE" the page, and post a comment as to what you enjoyed the most.

- Tweet "I recommend reading #Fallen by @annielobert of @hookersforjesus // @worthypub"

- Pick up a copy for someone you know who would be challenged and encouraged by this message.

- Write a book review online.

You can subscribe to Worthy Publishing's newsletter at
worthypublishing.com.

WORTHY PUBLISHING
FACEBOOK PAGE

WORTHY PUBLISHING
WEBSITE